Michael Rossonando

A FORGE OF
FREEDOM BOOK

0 50 100 200
MILES

N
W   E
S

Ticonderoga

N. H.

NEW
YORK

Albany

MASS.

Portsmouth
Boston
Plymouth

Hartford
CONN.
New Haven

R. I.

Newport
Providence

N. Y.

N. J.

New York City

PENNSYLVANIA

Trenton
Philadelphia *Burlington*
Wilmington

Baltimore
Annapolis

DEL.

MD.

MD.

VIRGINIA

Richmond
Williamsburg
Jamestown

NORTH CAROLINA

Charlotte *New Bern*

SOUTH
CAROLINA

Wilmington

Charleston

GEORGIA

Savannah

ATLANTIC OCEAN

The Thirteen Colonies
~1763~

RIKI

The Pennsylvania Colony

S.K. Stevens

CROWELL-COLLIER PRESS
Division of Macmillan Publishing Co., Inc.
New York
COLLIER MACMILLAN PUBLISHERS
London

Library of Congress Catalog Card Number: 73–97755

Macmillan Publishing Co., Inc.
866 Third Avenue, New York, N.Y. 10022
Collier Macmillan Canada, Ltd.
Printed in the United States of America

10   9   8   7   6 . 5   4   3

PICTURE CREDITS

Abby Aldrich Rockefeller Folk Art Collection, 38; The
Bettmann Archive, Inc., 76; Culver Pictures, Inc., 19, 79;
Pennsylvania Academy of Fine Arts, 34–35; Pennsylvania
Historical and Museum Commission; 10–11, 12, 30, 41, 48,
51, 53, 65, 66–67, 71, 74, 85, 89, 101, 108, 114; Philadelphia
Convention and Tourist Bureau, 110; Philadelphia Museum
of Art, 82

COVER ILLUSTRATION: *Independence Hall*

*To my three grandchildren,
who are good Pennsylvanians*

Contents

The Pennsylvania Colony

chapter 1

The First Pennsylvanians

In a sheltered place, along the high banks of the Juniata River not far from Huntington, archaeologists have found artifacts that show Indians lived in Pennsylvania at least eight thousand years before the birth of Christ. The first Indians may have come to North America over a strip of land which once joined it with Asia by way of the Bering Sea. Why they left Asia is not known, but it may have been in search of new sources of food. Over many thousands of years these people spread eastward as far as Pennsylvania. The first Indians to come to Pennsylvania were a primitive people, who knew nothing about farming and who hunted and fished for food, moving about to find new supplies of wild game.

Archaeological studies reveal that over the centuries the Indians in Pennsylvania very slowly improved their way of life. They began to plant and cultivate a unique grain which became known to white men as Indian corn, and learned how to dry it and store it in pots and baskets for later use. Although they grew corn and various other vegetables, such as pumpkin, they kept on hunting to obtain meat and hides for clothing.

Indians in the eastern United States, whatever their tribe or language, were very much alike in physical appearance, dress, customs, and way of life. In Pennsylvania there were two Indian groups, which differed from each other in their spoken language: the Algonkian (Al-gon-ki-an) and the Iroquoisan (Iro-qua-an). The Delaware were the major Algonkian tribe in Pennsylvania. The Indian name for these people was Lenni-Lenape (Len-ee Len-uh-pee). By the time the first white men came they were a settled and peaceful people. Their largest town was Shackamaxon (Shak-uh-mak-sun) at Germantown, where William Penn made his first treaty with the Indians. The largest early Iroquoisan tribe in Pennsylvania was known as the Susquehannocks because they lived mainly along the Susquehanna River from Maryland to as far as New York State.

Indian villages were located on the banks of streams and rivers because the land there was rich and because the Indians could travel along these waterways easily by canoe. In addition the Indians looked for good drinking water, good hunting grounds nearby, and a spot on the bank above flood level. Often a town was built within a wall or palisade of small tree trunks placed upright in the ground, creating a sort of fort for protection from enemy tribes. However, the Delaware Indians in southeastern Pennsylvania lived mostly in open villages without this protection because they were a peaceful tribe. A small village might have as few as six houses, but the larger ones, such as Shamokin near Sunbury, probably had several dozen.

These houses were built to accommodate several families. Called longhouses, they consisted of one room thirty or more feet long and about twenty feet wide. They were built by making a framework of small poles driven into the ground and tying the tops of the poles with roots and branches to other smaller and slimmer branches, which formed a flat roof. After the framework was complete, it was covered inside and out with overlapping sheets of tree bark, placed much as shingles are today on a house roof. Sometimes light poles or tree branches were also put on the outside of the bark sheets to make the house stronger.

Each family was assigned a particular portion of the longhouse and each had its own spot on the earth floor for a cooking fire. Openings in the roof allowed the smoke to escape. Although the Indians had no furniture, they did build sleeping bunks along the walls of their houses. As time went on, the Delaware began to build small one-family houses, oval in shape, but made of the same materials.

Land for farming was located outside the village. The Indians had learned to clear the land by an ingenious method. They killed the large trees by cutting a circle of bark around the trunk with a stone axe and then set them on fire. Women did the farm work because the men spent their time hunting and fishing for food—a natural division of labor. Using crude shorthandled hoes made by fastening a bone or other sharp object to a stick, the Indian women dug up enough loose soil to plant corn and other seeds. The corn was planted in small mounds of earth, and a few pumpkin or squash seeds usually were planted around them in the mound. Because their tools and methods limited the amount of land they could cultivate, we would probably call their planting gardening instead of farming, yet the ability to grow food even in this limited way allowed the Indians to give up the nomadic life they had led in earlier days.

Before the coming of Europeans to America the Indian had no domestic animal other than the dog. He did not know about the use of the wheel, nor did he know anything about the use of metal. The Indian of A.D. 1600 was a Stone Age man using stone to make the cutting point for tools or weapons such as the arrow or spear. After the white man came, the Indian traded skins for guns and metal hatchets or tomahawks, and metal pots for cooking, but he did not learn to use farm animals or the white man's cart or wagon.

In Indian families the mother rather than the father was the head. Children took their names from their mother's family rather than their father's. The idea that Indian women were almost slaves because they did hard work in the fields, tanned skins, and made them into clothing, while the men hunted, fished, or made war, is wrong. This was the Indian's way of dividing up the tasks women and men were best able to do.

Clothing was simple and suited to the Indian's way of life. Men wore a deerskin garment which covered the middle of the body. They added leggings when hunting to protect their lower legs from forest brush and brambles. Soft deerskin moccasins were good not only for walking long distances but also for quietly following game on the hunt. Women wore a loose dresslike garment, which came to about the knees, and moccasins. Indians in Pennsylvania did not wear the feather headdress seen on the Indians of the western plains. Can you imagine an Indian moving through the forest in such an outfit? The Pennsylvania Indian did wear a few feathers in his hair but only for special ceremonial dances.

Changes of season and the climate and weather were very important in the life of an Indian. His religion reflected this. It was based on worship of nature. His god was a Great Spirit who had made the world and everything in it. If hunting and crops were good, he believed he had pleased the Great Spirit. If they were bad, he had displeased him and tried to win back his favor. There were also lesser gods and spirits. Some tribes claimed the sun, the moon, or even the water or fire as their source of power and influence. At festivals such as the Green Corn Festival, celebrating the first ripe corn of the season, the Indian gave thanks to the gods with dances and ceremonies and he did the same when crops were harvested in the fall.

Because the Indians had no alphabet or written language, their knowledge was passed from one generation to another by spoken word or by example. There were no schools for Indian children. The history of the Indians existed almost entirely in stories passed on by older tribe members to the young over thousands of years. Sometimes important events were recorded as carvings on rocks or as designs in wampum belts. Knowledge of practical matters—hunting, fishing, planting, tanning hides, and such things as precautions and remedies against sickness—were learned from parents or other older Indians. Boys were taken on hunts to learn woodcraft and the art of hunting and girls learned cooking, planting, and other skills as well as the tribal legends and stories. Indian children seldom were punished. The skills they had to master were fairly simple and families lived closely together in an uncomplicated society, so perhaps there was no necessity for discipline.

The Indian had no formal government, though there were many customs which had to do with proper conduct or misconduct. Land was owned by the entire family. Its produce was shared within the family and even with the local tribe, which was made up of several families. Indians did not understand land ownership in the same way as the white men did, so that when the Indians made treaties selling land to white settlers they had one idea of the meaning of the treaty and the white men had another.

chapter 2

Early European Settlers

It was over a hundred years after Columbus reached the West Indies before Europeans learned about what is now Pennsylvania. Columbus and the explorers for Spain, Portugal, France, and England who followed were not interested in exploring the coast of America. They were intent on finding a northwest passage to India and the wealth of spices it held. Europeans were slow to realize that the New World held riches that would someday exceed those of the distant East.

The first explorers who came to Pennsylvania were the French. Jacques Cartier's exploration of the St. Lawrence River had led to the founding of New France, or Canada. Samuel de Champlain arrived and pushed on even farther. He founded a French settlement at Quebec in 1608. One of his men, Etienne Brulé, made a scouting trip to the upper Susquehanna River in northern Pennsylvania and reported on what he had seen to Champlain. Another great French explorer, Robert de La Salle, traveled all over the Great

Lakes region and is believed to have visited western Pennsylvania in his search for the source of the Ohio River.

But the French really only visited the Pennsylvania area. It was the Dutch who first fully explored the region and founded settlements in it. In the spring of 1609 the *Half-Moon,* under the flag of Holland and the Dutch East India Company, boldly headed toward the New World. Her captain was an Englishman named Henry Hudson. Hudson believed a passage to the Indies might be found below the area the French had explored. He visited Chesapeake Bay and the mouth of the Susquehanna River. Sailing northward, he entered Delaware Bay, which he called the South Bay. Hudson was one of the first explorers of the New World to keep a diary of his travels. He also brought back a cargo of valuable furs, which excited the merchants of the Dutch East India Company, who had begun to understand a little about the possible wealth of this new world

Eager for trade with this new land, the Dutch explored the Delaware River as far as the mouth of the Schuylkill River, which they named and which means "lower river" in Dutch. They built a fort on the east bank and started to trade with the Delaware Indians for furs. The Dutch flag was the first of three European flags to fly over the area around the lower Delaware. And a few Dutchmen were living in that region when Penn was given a grant to it by King Charles II of England in 1681.

At about this time in history the new nation of Sweden was building strength. In 1630, it had only about a million people and few resources, but it also had a warlike and able leader, King Gustavus Adolphus. He managed to build out of Sweden's tiny population one of the best armies in Europe and used it to gain from Russia control of Finland and part of Poland. After the king's death on the battlefield during his invasion of Germany, his young daughter Christina became queen and ruler of Sweden.

Gustavus Adolphus had long dreamed about colonies to make Sweden wealthy, and Queen Christina and her chancellor, Axel Oxenstierna, revived those dreams. A Dutchman, Peter Minuit, came to their aid. Earlier Minuit had been an explorer for his own country on the Delaware River. He knew, of course, that the Dutch already had forts and trading posts on the Delaware, but he was also aware that the Netherlands was growing weaker as a world power.

After consultation with Minuit the New Sweden Company was formed to trade and colonize in the New World, and the Delaware River basin was chosen as the place for the first settlement. Minuit helped raise Dutch money to finance the plan. Rich Dutchmen and Swedes put up money in the belief that they would reap profits from the fur trade and also from importing tobacco. Tobacco had been brought from the New World by the first Spanish explorers, and although the idea of smoking was completely new to Europeans, many liked it.

Late in 1637, after months of work, the first Swedish ships sailed for the New World. They were the *Kalmar Nyckel* and the *Fogel Grip* or *Gripen* under Minuit's command. Both ships were loaded with cloth and trinkets for trade with the Indians. Only a few settlers were on board, but they were well provisioned with tools such as axes and hoes, and wheat and other grain, which were to be used to start a settlement. Twenty-four Swedish soldiers were sent along to protect the new settlement. After a rough voyage on the stormy waves of the winter Atlantic, the ships sailed into the lower Delaware late in March, 1638. They proceeded up the bay to a small stream used by the Minqua Indians to transport their furs by canoe to the river. There the Swedes landed and Minuit fired a cannon and invited the Indians to a meeting with his men. A treaty was made to buy from the Indians a large tract of land along the river, but the Indians undoubtedly did not understand the meaning of the treaty because their idea of land ownership differed from that of white men. Some two miles up the stream, which the Swedes named the Christina after their young queen, a crude fort was built and it was also named for Christina. This fort was located at a point that came to be called the Rocks, part of present-day Wilmington, Delaware.

In June when Minuit set sail for Sweden in the *Kalmar Nyckel* he left behind the small group of settlers and soldiers to plant crops, hold the fort, and trade with the Indians for furs. Laden with furs Minuit's ship and the *Fogel Grip* returned by way of the West Indies, where the furs were exchanged for tobacco. Although Minuit died in a storm at sea, the Dutch ships sailed back to Sweden.

The men left behind in the fort were more soldiers than farmers. They nearly starved to death, and if the Indians had not helped them by showing them how to hunt and by selling them corn, they probably would have died. The second expedition to the settlement did not arrive until almost two years later, when in April, 1640, the *Kalmar Nyckel* returned. It brought more settlers and essential supplies such as tools and plows and some cattle. A tailor and a blacksmith were among the new arrivals, much needed skilled workers. A group of Dutch settlers arrived in November, 1640. In February, 1643, a fourth band of settlers with even more tools and cattle arrived and New Sweden's worst days were over.

This voyage brought Johan Printz, Queen Christina's new governor. Printz was a giant of a man nearly seven feet tall who weighed well over three hundred pounds. The Indians, quick to name persons on the basis of their appearance, called him "big body." For all his size, Printz was a capable man and he saw at once that a safer location for the fort and the capital of New Sweden would be farther up the Delaware. He decided on Tinicum Island, part of present-day Pennsylvania about twenty miles south of Philadelphia. At

Peter Minuit under the Swedish flag, sailed into the lower Delaware in March, 1638, laden with cloth and trinkets for trade with the Indians.

this new location a stronger fort was built, and a two-story log house, called Printzhof, for the governor. The new settlement also included a log church and school. This small fortified town was to become the first capital of Pennsylvania.

All might have been well if Johan Rising, who replaced Printz as governor in 1653, had not seized the Dutch fort

Casimir near Tinicum. The Dutch had maintained this weakened fort to protect their dwindling Indian fur trade, which they clung to, though much of it had been lost to the Swedes. It was the trade in furs which both the Dutch and Swedes sought as a main source of wealth. The Dutch governor at New Amsterdam was the hot-tempered Peter Stuyvesant, a veteran soldier. When Stuyvesant got the news of the attack on Fort Casimir he quickly sailed in September, 1655, for Tinicum with no less than seven ships carrying three hundred Dutch soldiers. The Swedish flag there was quickly lowered and that of New Netherlands raised. The four or five hundred Swedish and Finnish settlers there were allowed to keep their homes only after taking an oath of loyalty to the Dutch.

At the time of the Dutch seizure of New Sweden, England had colonies both north and south of this region. It was the only part of the Atlantic Coast from Canada to South Carolina over which an English flag did not fly. The former New Sweden, now a Dutch colony, was on land claimed by England, though it had been slow to explore the Delaware. Actually, the English captain Samuel Argall, in the ship aptly named the *Discovery*, dropped anchor the morn-

The newly appointed governor Johan Printz, whom the Indians called "big body," stood almost seven feet tall. He built Prinzhof, a small fortified town that became the first capital of Pennsylvania.

ing of August 27, 1610, in what he wrote was "a very great Bay." The Delaware Bay Indians from villages on the shore visited the *Discovery* in large numbers and Argall wrote that they were "very kind and promised me that the next day in the morning they would bring me a great store of Corne." This was more precious at the moment than furs because Argall was sailing for Virginia seeking food for starving Jamestown. It was Argall writing three years later who called the place "the De La Warre Bay," in honor of the Englishman Lord De La Warre, "Lord Governor & Captain Generall" of Virginia.

England's claim to all of North America dated as far back as Captain John Cabot's voyages for King Henry VII in 1497. The Netherlands and England were now at war as a result of rivalry over trade and mastery of the seas. Charles II of England sent a fleet and soldiers to seize New Amsterdam, the center of Dutch government. After capturing New Amsterdam, the English sent a small fleet down the coast, entered the Delaware, and forced the Dutch there to surrender their forts and lands. All of this was done without firing a shot. Few times in history was so much important land so easily taken in war. The Dutch later briefly regained control, but in 1674 the English regained and kept it.

Pennsylvania now had not only been discovered and explored but part of it had been settled. King Charles II gave the land on the Delaware to his brother the Duke of York, who set up a government for the region. The Swedes, Finns, and Dutch living there, about five hundred of them, then became English subjects. It must have been very hard for these people, mostly farmers, to keep track of just what allegiance to what government they were sworn to uphold. The land to the north of the Duke of York's grant was soon to be granted to William Penn by Charles II in payment for a debt the king owed to Penn's father's estate.

chapter 3

The Quakers, William Penn, and the Holy Experiment

Pennsylvania was unique among all the English colonies because from its very start it was a place where every person could worship God in his or her own way, and where all Christians had a right to take part in shaping their own government. The man who made this possible was William Penn and he called what he was trying to do in Pennsylvania a "holy experiment." It was indeed an experiment and it rested strongly upon Penn's religious ideals. As a young man Penn had become a member of an English religious group known as the Society of Friends. This group were called Quakers by many because one of their leaders once said they should always "quake before the power of the Lord."

The more formal title of Society of Friends was based on the Quakers' belief that all men are really friends and are completely equal in the eyes of God. More than a hundred years before Thomas Jefferson wrote the Declaration of

Independence, the Quakers practiced the ideal that all men are created equal and have such basic rights as life, liberty, and the pursuit of happiness. So strong was the Quaker belief in equality that they refused to remove their hats in court, or in the presence of high officials—even the king and queen—because they believed to do so was degrading and bowing down to vain titles. The Quaker love of his fellow-man included even his enemies, and a good Quaker was opposed to any form of violence. When he was young, Penn is said on one occasion to have been angered by a soldier heckling at a Quaker meeting. When Penn seized him by the collar to throw him out, an older Quaker said to Penn, "Let the man go in peace." The same thinking led the Friends to oppose war and to refuse to pay taxes for wars.

Unlike other Christians the Quakers had no ministers to interpret the Bible. They believed that every person could find moral guidance through an "Inner Light," the light of God that instructs a man's conscience. That is, a person's inner beliefs were the foundation of faith. Although they met together to worship in plain unadorned meeting houses, there was no preaching and no music. If a member felt inspired to share his thoughts and prayers, he rose and quietly addressed the congregation, but ordinarily Quakers worshiped in silence. This practice gave rise to the saying, "quiet as a Quaker meeting."

In all their habits the Quakers tried to live as simply as possible. Their simplicity grew out of their emphasis on spiritual values and their belief in the equality of men. Quaker dress was a plain, somber black or gray for both men and women. All bright colors, ornaments, and decorations were frowned upon. They rejected fancy clothing and showy possessions of all kinds because they felt such material possessions led men away from spiritual values and also served to indicate class distinctions.

Even their speech reflected their belief in the equality of

men. The upper class of that period used "you" for addressing an equal and "thou" for addressing a member of the
lower classes. As a protest against this distinction, the
Quakers used "thou" in speaking to one person of whatever
class and "you" only when speaking to a group. An English
aristocrat would have resented being spoken to in this
Quaker style and there is a story of the times that one such
aristocrat answered a Quaker by saying, "Why you ill-bred
clown. Don't you dare 'thou' me or I'll push 'thy' teeth
down 'thy' throat."

Quakers disapproved of music, dancing, play acting, and
most amusement. Anyone who entered a ballroom "cometh
forth a corrupt and wicked man." They agreed with Saint
Augustine that a dancer's steps were so many "leaps to hell."
They were warned also against "feastings and revellings"
and "banqueting." A Quaker who failed to live according to
this strict code might be called before the meeting to ex-
plain his or her sinful behavior and if not repentant might
be expelled from the meeting as punishment. At one meeting a group of young men were reprimanded for "galloping
and riding after an airy flurting manner" and lacking "mod-
eration and Gravity." In their austere moral and social con-
cepts the Quakers greatly resembled the New England Puritans but they were much more tolerant of the religious
beliefs of others than were their Puritan neighbors.

As the quiet and simple Quakers of Pennsylvania suddenly found their wealth increasing through commerce and
ownership of land, some of this austerity in dress and custom began to break down. A Quaker writing in 1760 com-
plained "marks of outward wealth" were beginning to appear in the dress and habits of Quakers, and as early as 1724,
the German printer Christopher Sauer noted that in Philadelphia "according to appearances plainness is vanishing
very much" even though "it is still noticcable in the clothes
except that the material is very costly, or is even velvet."

The Quaker faith was a part of the religious movement in Europe in the mid-seventeenth century known as Pietism because it placed emphasis upon simple Christian piety on the part of everyone. It was a revolt against the more formal beliefs of both the Catholic and Protestant religions, against their priests and ministers interpreting the Bible, and against their rituals and ceremonies. English Quakers did not differ very much in their basic religious ideas from the German Mennonites or Amish, a sect of the Mennonites. Peace with all men, simple ways of dress, speech, and religious practices were common to all these Pietist sects, which sought a return to early primitive Christianity. The founder of the Society of Friends in England in the 1650s was George Fox, a great English religious thinker, who became a friend and advisor of William Penn in his youth.

This was a time when every country had an established or state church which meant that one religious faith was in favor with the rulers and no other was tolerated. In Protestant England the established church was the Anglican Church, or the Church of England. No other faith was tolerated. Thus, the Quakers, who stood out from other Protestants of their day by not attending state churches, refusing to serve in the armed forces or to pay taxes for war, and refusing to pay homage to those in official positions, were greatly harassed and abused by those in authority. At this time, in the 1680s, England was at the peak of its harsh laws against dissent. The Quakers suffered most because they would not go underground but preached everywhere, even on the streets. "They go like lambs without any resistance," wrote Samuel Pepys, who has left us many glimpses of those times in his famous *Diary*. Pepys felt so badly about this persecution that he added, "I would to God they would either conform, or be more wise, and not be catched."

A short time before the Quaker religion was founded, William Penn was born in London on October 24, 1644. His father, also named William, was at only twenty-one a captain in the English navy, in the service of Charles I. When Charles I was deposed by Oliver Cromwell, Captain Penn continued to serve in the navy although his loyalties remained with the monarchy. Under Cromwell he quickly rose to the rank of admiral as a result of a great naval victory over the Dutch and became influential in naval affairs. In gratitude for Admiral Penn's successes, Cromwell awarded him estates in Ireland. It was while the family was visiting these estates that young William heard the Quaker leader Thomas Loe speak about his religious beliefs.

As a small boy William attended school near London and then studied under a private tutor. In 1660, the monarchy was restored under Charles II, and the elder Penn was knighted by the king for his continued loyalty. That same year, at the age of sixteen young William entered Christ Church College at Oxford, where his earlier interest in the Quaker religion was revived. Although his family was Anglican, Penn was attracted by the Quaker belief in the brotherhood of all men and their doctrine of the "Inner Light." At Oxford he refused to attend the required Anglican services and held prayer meetings with a group of friends. As a result he was fined and finally dismissed from Oxford.

As might be expected, Penn's father was shocked and dismayed by his son's behavior and took steps which he thought would take young William's mind off this nonsense. He put his son in both the army and the navy for short periods, and it was at this time that William Penn's only portrait was painted, *Penn in Armor,* which shows him as a young and good-looking soldier. This portrait is now in The Historical Society of Pennsylvania in Philadelphia. He was also sent to travel in Europe, where he took part in the lively social life of aristocratic circles. The one great mistake the admiral made was sending his son back to Ireland to look after the Penn lands—the teenage Penn again met Thomas Loe and

An engraving from Penn in Armor, *the only portrait painted of William Penn, shows him as a handsome young soldier.*

in 1667 received what he called his "convincement" as a Quaker.

Penn returned to England from his stay in Ireland a devoted Quaker and it was not long before he began to feel the consequences. He was arrested with William Mead for preaching as a Quaker on a London street. Their meeting house had been closed because the government did not tolerate Quaker preaching. The two were held in what Penn called a "noisome and stinking" jail for two weeks before they were brought to court in what became a very famous trial. Penn, who refused in Quaker fashion to remove his hat in court and argued much, was called a "saucy fellow" by the presiding officer. When the jury found Penn and Mead not guilty, the court refused to accept the verdict. The judge ordered them thrown back into jail and even ordered that the jury be fined and jailed. Penn argued strongly for the right of a jury not to be so treated and in the end won his point. The case is a landmark in English law because of the defense of the right of trial by jury.

This was not the last time Penn was arrested and jailed for preaching Quaker beliefs. He was thrown into Newgate Prison a year later and this time was not given a jury trial. Penn told the judge, "I scorn the religion which is not worth suffering for." He refused to allow his father or friends to try to secure his release from prison, which they could have done because of their friends in high places. Using his time in prison to write letters and pamphlets defending freedom of conscience and the ideals of the Friends, Penn became a welcome and much needed leader of the Quakers, who were generally from the poorer class of shopkeepers and workers. Because of his superior education and his acquaintanceship with the Stuart kings, he was able to receive a hearing for the Quaker view, when other Quakers would have been ignored or mistreated. He was a young and vigorous leader and after a time became known as the most capable preacher and writer among the Quakers.

However, in spite of Penn's efforts, the Quakers continued to suffer persecution and many of them began to think about emigrating to the New World. Some went to Long Island, then under Dutch control, because the Dutch were known for their religious toleration, but unexpectedly they were also persecuted there. Finally, a group of Quakers including William Penn purchased land in West Jersey, now a part of New Jersey. According to many sources, Penn drafted the liberal and democratic constitution for the Jersey colony.

Inspired by his involvement with the West Jersey settlements and disturbed by the continued persecution of the Quakers in England, Penn began to think of setting up a colony of his own. In this new colony he would see to it that freedom of religion and the right of the people to self-government would have full protection. He applied to Charles II for a grant of land in the New World. King Charles was glad to approve the request because England had control of the entire Atlantic seaboard down to Florida except for the Pennsylvania-Delaware area. A new colony would make her control almost complete. Also, the king owed Penn's father a sizeable sum, about $100,000 in today's money. This money was now due Penn because his father had died and Penn had inherited his estate. Since it was much easier for the king to pay the debt in land than in money, Penn secured a charter early in 1681 for a colony of some forty thousand square miles of land, an area three-fourths as large as England. The original charter is now displayed in a specially built case in the Memorial Hall of the William Penn Memorial Museum in Harrisburg, Pennsylvania.

The story of how Pennsylvania got its name is interesting. Penn wanted to name his colony New Wales because like Wales it was "a pretty hilly country." The secretary to the Privy Council, a Welshman, objected. For some reason he resented naming a new and unknown country after Wales. Penn then suggested Sylvania, because of the area's woodlands. At the king's request this was changed to "Pennsilvania," "a name the king would give it in honour of my father," wrote Penn.

Penn began at once to plan for the government of his colony. He was full of ideas for making it a place where the people would have a real voice in the government. To the very first settlers, he wrote that "it hath pleased God in his Province to cast you within my lot and care" and "you shall be governed by laws of your own making, and live a free and if you will, a sober and industrious life."

He gave much of his time the next year to writing a First Frame of Government, a constitution, which began with mention of "the great and wise God," who had made the world. Penn truly wanted his colony to be a "holy experiment."

At the same time, he set about writing pamphlets to tell Europeans about his new lands and to invite them as settlers. In the pamphlets he wrote about the rich soil and fine climate of Pennsylvania. He went about selling his land with the same ardor he had sold Quakerism. It is a "goodly land," said Penn. What he wrote about Pennsylvania must have sounded very fine to poor European farmers, most of whom were landless and worked for a bare living on estates belonging to the nobility. Penn was not able to go to Pennsylvania for a year after receiving his charter and sent instead his cousin, Sir William Markham, a British army captain, as deputy governor.

chapter 4

Seed of a Nation

The United States grew from seeds of liberty and freedom planted in the Thirteen Colonies, starting with the founding of Virginia in 1607 and ending with Georgia in 1732. William Penn wrote to a Quaker friend soon after King Charles II granted his charter that "my God . . . will, I believe bless and make it the seed of a nation. . . ." This was a thought deep in Penn's mind as he developed his ideas on how Pennsylvania should be governed.

Early in the fall of 1682 three ships were leaving for Pennsylvania and William Penn made plans to sail on one of them, the *Welcome*. About a hundred Quaker settlers were also on board. The illness of Penn's wife Gulielma, whom he fondly called Guli, made it impossible for her and the children to sail with him. Penn was thirty-eight, a slim, handsome, vigorous man who was not at all drab or Quakerish. He was very fond of riding and took with him three of his finest horses.

This sailing must have been very exciting for Penn and his fellow Quakers, but to the *London Gazette* for September 2, 1682, it was worth only this note: "Two days since sailed out of the *Downs* three ships bound for *Pensilvania* on board of which was Mr. Pen, with a great many Quakers who go to settle there." They took with them cows, chickens, and settlers' furnishings. The voyage was full of hardship. Smallpox hit the *Welcome* and thirty-one died in a week. Fortunately, Penn was immune because of a childhood attack of the disease and he spent most of the voyage nursing the sick. It was a rough seven weeks before the vessel reached land at Egg Harbor, New Jersey, and it was three days more before the *Welcome* reached the Dutch and Swedish settlement at New Castle on the Delaware River. This was then a Pennsylvania port because the Duke of York, who had had title to the region, had turned it over to Penn late in August. It is now in Delaware.

At New Castle Penn first heard himself called governor. The settlers there gave him a bit of earth, a twig, and some river water in a little flask as a symbol of his owning the land. Penn then sailed up the Delaware to the tiny Swedish town known as Upland, where he was warmly greeted. He asked a sailor, "What would thou call this place?" The man was from Chester, England, and said he thought this would be a good English name for the town. Penn agreed and that is how Chester got its name and became Pennsylvania's oldest English town. Despite Penn's enthusiasm a fellow Quaker on board was not much impressed by this new land and he wrote a little peevishly that it was a "wilderness; the chief inhabitants were Indians and some Swedes." Penn moved farther up the Delaware in a six-oared barge and landed at the foot of Dock Creek at what he called his new "greene countrie town" of Philadelphia, which had been laid out in 1682 on his orders.

The first thing Penn did was to ask the settlers to elect

from among them an assembly to represent them in the government. This assembly was to consist of not over two hundred men and was to be elected annually. The Pennsylvania legislature even today is called the General Assembly. The first Assembly met at Chester, December 4, 1682, and a second met in March, 1683, in the new town of Philadelphia. A Provincial Council composed of seventy-two men was also elected. Presided over by the governor, this council proposed the laws that were then submitted to the Assembly for a vote.

William Penn had brought with him a constitution for the colony, which he called the First Frame of Government. He did not believe this should be the final version of the constitution because he was aware that the needs and desires of the people would change. He continually consulted the people about what they wanted. The people did have ideas and through their elected Assembly they presented them to Penn. As a result a Second Frame of Government was adopted at Philadelphia in April, 1683, which gave the people more power through the elected Assembly, and limited that of the governor.

William Penn is looked upon today as a truly great man because he was willing to accept such limits on his authority. As governor appointed by the king and also the original owner of all the land, he could have rejected any limits on his authority. Instead, he listened patiently at all times to those who presented sound new ideas of increasing the power of the people, and he approved them. Some of the members of the Assembly wanted the power to propose laws instead of just voting a "yes" or "no" on those which were drawn up by the governor's Council. This idea was voted down because some members said it seemed ungrateful to Penn "for his Goodness towards the People." Pennsylvanians already had far more liberty and right to take part in their government than did Englishmen at home but not everyone was satisfied. However, it was not until 1701 that a third constitution, known as the Charter of Privileges, was adopted.

In the meantime Philadelphia began to grow and flourish. Ships arrived there loaded with settlers. There were soon some eighty houses in the town, and at least three hundred farms around it. By 1700 Philadelphia was for that day a small city of about four thousand people. It grew so rapidly that houses could not be built fast enough and some settlers had to dig caves in the clay banks of the Delaware for temporary homes.

Pennsylvania was America's first true melting pot of people of various ethnic patterns. There were Swedes, Dutchmen, and Finns, along with some Englishmen living along the lower Delaware when Penn came in 1682. Those who came in the next few years were mostly English Quakers but some Welsh Quakers also arrived. They had bought land from Penn and called it the Welsh Barony. Such names as Bryn Mawr and Gwynedd are reminders of this Welsh settlement. The first Germans who came were led by Francis Daniel Pastorius, and were Quakers and Mennonites who had many beliefs in common. Pastorius was head of the Frankford Land Company, which bought some of Penn's land. When they arrived in 1683 they settled at a place they named Germantown.

Penn was kept very busy on his first visit to Pennsylvania. In addition to deciding on matters of government, and to overseeing much of the growth of Philadelphia, he spent many hours with the Indians making treaties for land. He surprised some of his fellow Quakers by entertaining Indian leaders for dinner at his Philadelphia house. Pastorius said the Indians "loved and praised" Penn. He was so fit and vigorous that he once challenged an Indian to a foot race and won with ease.

Soon Penn had to return to England because Maryland's

governor, Lord Baltimore, was questioning Penn's right to much of southern Pennsylvania. Lord Baltimore claimed this area under Maryland's earlier charter. The problem arose because no one knew anything about the geography of the New World. Early charters from English kings always granted lands from "sea to sea," without any clear statement of just what this meant. Boundary lines north or south were vague and inaccurate. Since Pennsylvania was the next to the last colony for which a charter was granted it naturally became a victim of boundary disputes. It had boundary troubles not only with Maryland but later with Connecticut and Virginia.

Before leaving Philadelphia, Penn composed a farewell prayer for the city. He wrote: "Philadelphia, the virgin settlement of this province, named before thou wert born, what love, what care, what service, and what travail has there been to bring thee forth and preserve thee from such as would abuse and defile thee." He prayed that his city of brotherly love "mayest be kept from the evil that would overwhelm thee; that, faithful to the God of thy mercies, in the life of righteousness, thou may be preserved to the end." He ended his prayer with the words, "the God of eternal strength keep and preserve thee to his glory and peace."

It was on October 6, 1684, a little more than two years after he had left England, that William Penn in the tiny ship *Endeavor* dropped anchor on the Sussex coast at a village just about seven miles from his home. He greeted his wife Guli, thin from her long illness; and seven-year-old Springett, his eldest son; young William; and his daughter Letitia, who was called Tishe. They were happy to see Penn, and the children undoubtedly were full of curiosity about the distant Pennsylvania from which he came. After a short time Penn had to leave for London to see the king.

Penn wrote that he was "received very graciously" by the ailing Charles II, who died early in 1685. His successor,

James II, spoke of Penn as a "singular and entire friend." Although James was a Catholic, Penn hoped to use his personal friendship to obtain the freedom of several hundred Quakers in England who were in prison because of their beliefs. As a result of Penn's efforts and those of other advocates of religious toleration, James issued a general pardon in 1686 for members of all religious faiths in prison. Some of those released had not seen the sun for fifteen years.

In 1688 England staged its Glorious Revolution, which drove James II of the Stuart family from the throne and replaced him with Protestant William of Orange as king and his wife Mary, daughter of James II, as queen. Penn's close friendship with James II made William and Mary doubtful of his loyalty. Late in 1693 they prohibited him from taking any part in governing Pennsylvania but he was allowed to keep his lands. In just about a year his governorship was returned to him. During that year Penn was in hiding, fearing he might be arrested for treason.

Five years later, Penn returned to Pennsylvania, leaving England on September 9, 1699. His wife Guli had died and Penn had remarried. He brought with him his second wife, Hannah Callowhill Penn, his daughter Letitia, and his son Springett. Penn's return was necessary because affairs had not been going at all well in the colony. The people were clamoring for even more rights in the governing body. Penn set himself to answer these demands. Penn's very presence helped sooth the differences. James Logan, who came with him and became one of his closest advisors, wrote, "Friends love to the governor was great and sincere; they had long mourned for his absence, and passionately desired his return. He, they firmly believed, would compose all their differences and repair all that was amiss. . . ."

Penn listened patiently to what the people had to say. The outcome was Penn's last constitution for Pennsylvania in 1701. Early in 1699 he told the Assembly, "Yet wee have much to do to make a free Constitution, and the Courts of Justice therein." He went on to say, "Friends—If in the Constitution by Charter there be anything that jarrs—alter it. If you want a law for this or that, prepare it. . . ." No person could have told the people more clearly that he wanted them to have the greatest freedom to alter the government.

It is not always easy for men to act together in harmony. Members of the Pennsylvania Assembly found it difficult to agree on what new laws were needed. Much debate finally led Penn to write The Charter of Privileges Granted by William Penn, Esquire; To the Inhabitants of Pennsylvania and Territories in 1701, better known simply as the Charter of Privileges. It said that freedom of conscience was man's most precious liberty and no persons who acknowledged "one Almighty God" should be "compelled to frequent or maintain any Religious Worship, Place or Ministry, contrary to their Mind. . . ." Any persons who "also profess to believe in Jesus Christ" could "Serve this Government in any capacity." Of course, this prevented Jews from holding an office, but Jews were welcome and did come. An Assembly made up of members from each county elected yearly by the freemen, the citizens who met the property requirements to vote, was given the power to prepare and pass all laws. The people also were now given the right to elect a number of persons from whom the governor would appoint such local officials as sheriffs. This charter went so far in new ideas of liberty that it was put on the famous Freedom Train which toured the nation when Franklin D. Roosevelt was President showing the people the greatest documents in the history of our freedoms. One great American historian has called it "the most famous of all colonial constitutions." Its ideas influenced the thinking of the men who later wrote the Declaration of Independence in 1776 and framed the Constitution of the United States in 1787.

Right, William Penn's restored study in Pennsbury manor where he wrote much of the Charter of Privileges in 1701. Below, restored Pennsbury manor on the Delaware as it looks today.

Penn hardly had time to sign this great document, much of which must have been drawn up in his study at his new home at Pennsbury on the Delaware, before he had to set sail for England. Political affairs there were again in turmoil and he wanted to be on hand to prevent possible loss of the colony to the Crown. Once there he found he was in the best graces of the new queen, "good Queen Anne," as she was known, who came to the throne in 1702 and had known him as the close friend of her father King James II.

Although his relationship with the Crown was good, he now found himself in serious difficulties. The cost of founding and getting Pennsylvania started as a colony had been great. Furthermore, some of the men who had kept his accounts had been dishonest. Sale of land had not brought Penn much wealth. He was in debt and it was so serious that he was actually thrown into prison for debt. He stayed in prison almost a year until Quaker friends raised money to pay his debts and get him out.

The people in the colony seemed never to be satisfied with what they had gained in the way of free government and with their growing well-being. Penn was so troubled he once wrote to them, "Friends. The eyes of many are upon you. The people of many nations of Europe look on that country [Pennsylvania] as a land of ease and quiet, wishing themselves in vain the same blessings . . . you enjoy." At one time he thought of selling Pennsylvania to Queen Anne but he was afraid the people might lose some of their freedom and so despite his desperate need for money he did not do so.

Penn was now sixty-five years old but he kept on writing Quaker sermons and pamphlets and hundreds of letters to many Friends until his health finally broke down and he died on July 30, 1718. Even the Indians on the Delaware mourned for him. His widow, Hannah Penn, a rather stern and forceful woman, became owner and governor of Pennsylvania until her death in 1727. Hannah Penn was Pennsylvania's only woman governor. Following English law, her three sons, John, Thomas, and Richard Penn shared the ownership of the land and the governorship. It was not until 1775 that Penn's grandson John finally became sole owner of the Penn lands, just in time to lose them to the new state of Pennsylvania in the Revolution. None of Penn's sons had his wisdom or his true interest in Pennsylvania, and all of them left the Quaker faith to become members of the Anglican Church. Yet their father had left to them what was truly the "seed of a nation" and from this seed Pennsylvania kept on growing.

chapter 5

Those Who Came

After Penn created in Pennsylvania a land where people could enjoy religious liberty and a chance to take part in an experiment in self-government, many thousands of settlers came to share in the promise of this new freedom and opportunity. It is important to know about those who came because the life and culture they brought with them and adapted to their new homeland shaped that of Pennsylvania for many years to come. Descendants of these early comers became and are even today leaders in every phase of Pennsylvania life.

Why did these people come? That is a question not easily answered. The reasons can be learned only by studying the different peoples who did come and the conditions in their homelands which influenced them to leave. Some persons wanted religious freedom while others wanted a better chance to make a living as a farmer or laborer. Still others liked the idea of more freedom to take part in the

*Artist Benjamin West portrayed
William Penn's peacemaking
ability in his famous*
Penn's Treaty with the Indians.

government and escape from the often harsh rule of a European king, which often included forced service in the army. Often it was a combination of these factors. Probably a desire for more religious freedom was mixed with a longing for a better life and a measure of political freedom in the motivation of most of the Europeans who came to Pennsylvania by the thousands in the 1700s.

From the start Pennsylvania became a meeting place for people from many parts of Europe. This was what Penn wanted because he was not only building a new kind of colony in the New World but at the same time he was very much a real estate agent selling land. Once a European

bought a plot of land he still faced the problem of getting from his old home in Europe to his new home in Pennsylvania. This was not easy and it is difficult today to understand just how hard it was to make such a change. People now think nothing of moving thousands of miles to a new home and job but two hundred years ago when our forefathers faced such a move it required a great deal of courage. Hardly any European who came to Pennsylvania had ever been more than a few miles from his home. He was in all likelihood either a poor tenant farmer on a noble's estate or a lowly shopkeeper in some town bound to a trade guild, or even a servant of some noble. And if one stops to think about the dangers and hardships it is a wonder that anyone was brave enough to try to come to the New World, even with the promise that Pennsylvania seemed to offer. Our ancestors must have burned with desire for a better life in this new land.

Once the decision to come was made, other problems had to be faced such as getting to a seaport where there was a ship of passage. Then there was the question of paying for passage on the ship. Many of these people were so poor they could not pay in money and so they agreed to work when they arrived in Philadelphia for any person who would pay the money to redeem their ship fare. They were called bond servants or redemptioners. Sometimes even children were bound out for service, almost like Negro slaves. Their serv-ices were often sold to the highest bidder in Philadelphia, though they received better treatment than the slaves and only had to work long enough to pay their debt, which was apt to be about five years. It is difficult today to imagine the hardships faced by a shipload of these immigrants. The trip across the stormy Atlantic could take as many as twelve weeks and the small ships were crowded with just as many people and their belongings as the owner could squeeze into the space he had. The ship carried as little food and water as possible in order to hold more people, and if storms de-layed a voyage the supply sometimes ran short. Sometimes farm animals were crowded into the same ship. The food was salt meat, coarse bread, and that was about all. Scurvy, caused by lack of fruit and vegetables, was common. Also with people huddled together smallpox sometimes broke out on ships and one shipload of one hundred and fifty people from Germany is said to have lost all but fifty pas-sengers from that and other diseases.

Many of those who survived such voyages, and who could write, sent home letters that overlooked the hardships. They were so excited by the bright new land of freedom and a chance for a new and better life ahead of them that they forgot all earlier trouble. Few who came ever advised others not to come. The contrast of life in early Pennsylvania with the hard and unyielding life of the European peasant and town worker was so great as to overcome any remaining doubts about coming to Penn's new land of promise. Benjamin Franklin summed it up very well when he wrote that there were "few people so miserable as the poor of Europe" and pointed out that land was so cheap in Pennsylvania and so productive that the poorest early settler could in a few years become wealthy by European standards.

It was only natural that those who came first were mostly English Quakers who knew about Penn and the promise of religious toleration he offered. Penn sold several hundred thousand acres of land to Quakers before he came to Pennsylvania. The price he put on his land was five pounds (about twenty-five dollars) for a hundred acres. These first Quakers came mainly from the larger English towns and included tradesmen such as carpenters and shoemakers. They were glad to come not only to find relief from the bitter persecution they suffered in England but also a chance for higher income. Once Pennsylvania was growing, many Quakers came from other colonies where they could not worship without fear of persecution. The Puritans in New England did not want them at all and in Massachusetts six Quakers were actually put to death. New Englanders generally made life uncomfortable for Quakers, who could not vote or take part in the government. Thus, Penn's new colony looked very good to those few Quakers who had tried to find a new life elsewhere. The southeastern counties of Philadelphia, Bucks, and Chester were the centers of Quaker settlement, and these counties became the leaders in political and business affairs and shaped the cultural life of early Pennsylvania. Quaker influence, which lasted even after other groups of people came in large numbers, resulted in a

This folk art painting by a Quaker artist is believed to be typical of the people, their dress, animals and buildings on a Pennsylvania farm during the Revolutionary period.

certain austerity and plainness which some think persist even today. Other Englishmen, mostly non-Quakers, came to Pennsylvania later but not in any large numbers.

In Germany Penn's success in selling land was remarkable. It was the result of certain conditions which existed there in the early 1700s. There was then no German nation and the Germanies, as the area was known, was made up of a large number of small kingdoms and principalities. It was the last part of central Europe to retain the feudal system. Under this system peasants were almost slaves, who lived and worked to enrich the landholders while getting a mere hand-to-mouth existence for themselves. Furthermore, the entire area had been ravaged by thirty years of war from 1618 to 1648. Rival European armies had fought back and forth across the land so often that even the best of it was in a sad state. The Protestant revolt against the Catholic Church had taken place in Germany in the 1500s and there were still bitter religious conflicts there. Each kingdom had its own favored religion which was the only one tolerated. Also, every male peasant was subject to military service at the call of his ruler. Life was indeed hard for most German peasants. It is not surprising that they responded so eagerly to Penn's message: "Come to my province of Pennsylvania where you will find land you can own yourself, peace, freedom for worship in your own way, and a chance to take part in governing yourselves." Germans came by the thousands after about 1720 and soon numbered about one-half the population of Pennsylvania.

These thousands of Germans were of many different religions. The Mennonites, led by Pastorius, who came with the first Quakers, have been mentioned. The Amish, who came a little later, were a small band of people who had broken away from the Mennonites. Both were known for their simple piety and plain dress and were not much different in their beliefs from the English Quakers. They were simple farm folk and did not stay in Philadelphia but moved inland where farm land could be had. The Amish were truly the plain people who worshiped in their homes without ministers, frowned on schools, dressed in plain black or gray clothing, and kept to themselves in their own small farm communities, as they do even today. Another small sect called Moravians settled Bethlehem in 1740, their center in America. They were unlike the other sects and less plain in their ideas and faith but were known for their zeal in trying to convert the Indian to Christianity. But by far the larger number of German immigrants belonged to the organized churches, the Reformed and the Lutheran.

Most of the German settlers came from what was known as the Palatinate along the Rhine River and were farmers or skilled craftsmen. In central Pennsylvania, in the region which became Berks, Lehigh, Northampton, Lebanon, and Lancaster counties, they found rich farm land in a setting much like their native Rhineland and this is where they built their new homes. Since the German word for German is *Deutsch,* most English-speaking people called them simply "Dutch"; they soon became known as Pennsylvania Dutch, as they still are. Although they continued to speak German, many English words crept into their language and from it grew a sort of language known as Pennsylvania Dutch and there was even a Pennsylvania Dutch literature. The fact that these Germans went on speaking their native language helped keep alive a common Germanic culture for generations, but it also led to some problems in their relations with other early settlers. Since a German-speaking settler did not always understand what was said to him in English some thought he was ignorant and the term "dumb Dutch" came into use by his neighbors.

Most Pennsylvania Germans were farmers and they were far from ignorant. They helped to make Pennsylvania very prosperous in colonial days because they grew valuable farm crops such as wheat, which was very important in colonial commerce. They built fine farm buildings which visitors to colonial America thought were the best anywhere. The Moravians were famous for their early great religious choral music for voices and wind instruments, and much early American music of a religious nature can be traced back to these German settlers in Pennsylvania. Germans are hearty eaters and these settlers reproduced in America their favorite foods from the Old World: sauerkraut, a great variety of sausages made from pork, such things as liver pudding and cottage cheese, and *schnitz und knepp,* or dried apples and dumplings. Most Germans looked well fed and "as round and jolly as a Pennsylvania Dutchman" became a common saying.

The Pennsylvania Germans liked to decorate things in color, even their barns, but especially their household furniture. They used more or less common symbols in decorating, among which the lily is very evident. The decorations on barns have been called "hex signs" because other settlers thought they were used to drive away evil spirits. But the Pennsylvania Germans painted their barns out of simple love of color and decoration. Art of this kind was the work of the common people and it has come to be known as folk art. Pennsylvania German folk art is highly prized and eagerly sought by collectors. Germans made much of cele-

The Pennsylvania Germans painted elaborate decorations on their barns and furniture. Some of the favorite symbols were the peacock and the tulip.

brating Christmas and the settlers introduced German Christmas customs to this country. With the exception of the Mennonites and the Amish plain people, the German settlers were rather lively and their love of music and art was a pleasant contrast in the colonial population to the rather drab and austere Quakers and the stern Presbyterianism of the Scotch-Irish.

The Scotch-Irish were yet a third major group of people who came to colonial Pennsylvania seeking freedom. They were actually Scots who had been persuaded by English rulers to move from their native Scotland into northern Ireland in the belief these hardy Scotch Presbyterians would offset the influence of the Catholic Irish in the south. The Scottish were promised land and freedom of worship in Ireland but they found little of either. They were soon persecuted for being Presbyterians instead of Church of England people and the English landlords kept raising the rent on land. Failure of crops in northern Ireland in the 1700s increased their difficulties and by 1720 the Scotch-Irish began to come to Pennsylvania by way of Philadelphia in search of a new chance to make their dreams come true.

Since the Germans had already bought up most of the best farm land in eastern Pennsylvania, the Scotch-Irish had to move farther to the west. They liked the mountains of western Pennsylvania because they were much like those in Scotland and northern Ireland. The very early Scotch-Irish settled in northern Lancaster County and later arrivals moved up into the region of present-day Dauphin and Cumberland counties. They were the first to settle beyond the Allegheny Mountains in any number.

By the eve of the American Revolution there were at least seventy thousand of these "Irish" in the colony and the English Quakers were wondering whether Ireland was not sending "all its inhabitants thither." A rough and ready people used to hardship in their north Ireland homes, they were not afraid to tackle life on the Pennsylvania frontier. They chopped down trees, built their log cabins, planted their small farms on the land cleared from the forested wilderness, and fought Indians when necessary—all with equal gusto. The Quaker government in Philadelphia thought this was very fine until the Scotch-Irish, sometimes called the "wild Irish," began to take land without bothering to buy it from the Penn family or paying any attention to Indian rights. It was often said that the Scotch-Irish carried with them a Bible, a gun, a knife, and a willingness to fight at the drop of a coonskin cap. Almost all of them were Presbyterians and though they were thought by some people in the eastern part of the province to be wild if not uncivilized they were quick to build churches and also schools. They took to politics as the duck does to water and had a fierce love of liberty. They were among the first settlers to oppose England in the battle over taxation without representation which led to the American Revolution. A Hessian soldier in the British army during the Revolution is said to have written home that it was really "a Scotch-Irish uprising." Since they were Presbyterians, their faith and their culture were somewhat austere and they frowned on frivolity almost as much as did Quaker Philadelphia.

The English, German, and Scotch-Irish were the largest groups to come to Pennsylvania in search of a new way of life, but there was a sprinkling of others. French Huguenots, who were members of the Protestant faith forced to flee France because of religious persecution after 1685, came in some numbers by way of Germany. Some French and Irish Catholics came too, because even though Maryland was a Catholic colony, Pennsylvania promised a better chance to improve their living conditions. Jewish settlers came in search of greater opportunities in trade and commerce and even though they could not vote or hold office they became key leaders in business and financial life and some headed trade companies.

It is clear that those who came to Pennsylvania in colonial days did so for several reasons, and often the reasons must have been mixed. There was so little freedom of any kind in Europe at that time that Pennsylvania must have loomed in the eyes of many as the one place where it could be found in all its forms.

chapter 6

Daniel Boone and
the Pennsylvania Frontier

In the history of the United States, the word "frontier" has
been used to locate an imaginary line marking the edge of a
region where settlers had farms and homes and separating
it from the wilderness just beyond. Much of the early history
of our country is the story of how this frontier moved stead-
ily inland and westward after the time that the first Englishmen landed on the shores of the Atlantic and began their
settlements at Jamestown and Plymouth. Pennsylvania's first
frontier was where the first settlements along the Delaware
faded into the wilderness. It was a frontier pushed farther
and farther into central Pennsylvania and finally into the
lands beyond the Allegheny Mountains just before the Revolution.

The frontier was always a moving line because the first
Americans were a people hungry for land. From the days
when the first settlements in Pennsylvania were huddled
along the Delaware there were those who thought about the

untouched rich land beyond. In early Pennsylvania this often meant moving no more than a hundred miles or so, but it was always a little farther into the wilderness. Since those who came to Pennsylvania needed real courage and hardihood even to start their journey to the New World it is easy to understand why they were not afraid to move again.

The Indian stood in the way of this push and though William Penn had tried to protect the red man and keep the peace, his sons, who inherited Pennsylvania, cared little about the Indians. They did continue to make treaties with them and to make a token purchase of their land. There were over thirty such treaties made before the Revolution, all of them signed by the Indian chiefs who pledged to observe them "as long as the creeks and rivers run, and while the sun, the moon, and the stars endure." Since the Indians had a different idea of land ownership from the white man's, believing that they still had hunting and fishing rights no matter who owned the actual land, they did not understand what these treaties would lead to. Thus, when the white settlers fenced off the land and denied the Indians hunting and fishing rights, trouble broke out.

Penn's sons did not help the cause of peace when they fooled the Indians in the famous Walking Purchase of 1737. Certain chiefs had once told William Penn they would sell him a piece of land running from a place in Bucks County north "as far as a man can walk in a day and a half." This would have been about twenty-five miles, but Penn's sons hired three special walkers, who instead of walking actually ran in relay fashion and so covered about sixty miles. As a result of this fraudulent maneuver, many Indians were now forced from their homes and moved to the upper Susquehanna Valley in northeastern Pennsylvania. But they were soon driven from that region by white settlers who had come down from Connecticut believing this land a part of their colony under their earlier charter. The Delaware and Shawnee Indians who were thus made victims of the white man's trickery and greed were pushed into western Pennsylvania and the Ohio country. From there they later fought back in savage raids on the Pennsylvania frontier.

Three years before the Walking Purchase was accomplished, Daniel Boone was born, on November 2, 1734, in a log house on the Berks County frontier. Daniel Boone became the most famous pioneer and wilderness scout in our early history and the first sixteen years of his life spent on the Pennsylvania frontier were typical of the pioneer life of those times.

The Boone family story is typical of the hunger for land which brought people to Pennsylvania and then led them westward. The Boones were Quakers and Daniel's grandfather, George Boone, heard in his native England about William Penn's new province where Quakers could live and worship without fear. Uncertain of what to expect of the New World he did a rather unusual thing. He sent his three eldest children ahead to Pennsylvania about 1713 to look at the new country. One of these was Squire Boone, Daniel's father, another was George, and, surprisingly, the last was their sister, Sarah. After they had looked over Pennsylvania, all three returned to England and told their father it was a good land. As a result, in late September, 1717, George Boone and his family landed at Philadelphia seeking a new home. The Boones first settled about twelve miles north of Philadelphia but soon moved another dozen miles farther north and west, and in just a little while moved yet a third time farther west into the Oley Valley in present Berks County.

The Oley region was on the edge of the new frontier just opened to settlement and only a few familes had moved there. There was plenty of wild game such as deer and bear in the heavily forested rolling hills, and there was abundant

Daniel Boone, pioneer and wilderness scout, spent his early years in Pennsylvania. He may have looked very much like this scout with his long Pennsylvania rifle.

fish in the Manatawny and Monocacy Creeks as well as the nearby Schuylkill River leading to Philadelphia, and there were even a few beavers for fur. No roads had been laid in this still wild country and the settlers used the Indian trails. The old Shawnee Path from Philadelphia northward ran right through the center of the Oley region which had been the home of the Shawnee Indians until about 1732 when the Penns bought the land from them. There is no doubt that as a young boy Daniel Boone saw some of these Shawnee, who lived not far away and continued to use the old trails. He may also have seen and even known such noted frontiersmen as Conrad Weiser, the great Indian interpreter, and George Croghan, known as the "prince of Indian traders," both of whom loomed large in the history of the Pennsylvania frontier.

There was peace in their frontier territory, and since most of the settlers were Quakers, this peaceful relationship between the white men and the red men was generally stable. But in 1728, there were rumors, which Daniel's grandfather relayed to Governor Patrick Gordon at Philadelphia, that the Indians "will fall upon us very suddenly." He urged that guns and powder be sent because otherwise "we shall undoubtedly perish and our province be destroyed." There was in fact a brush between Indians and settlers but nothing approaching what George Boone had feared. The outcome was one Indian wounded, no whites harmed.

The Boones were not the first white men in the Oley Valley. There had been some pioneers there as early as 1712. These were undoubtedly the kind of people typical of the very early frontier who were hunters and trappers more than farmers. Often wild and reckless, these frontiersmen had seized the land they held before Penn had time to buy it from the Indians. Caring nothing about who owned the land, they squatted on it, living much like the Indians. These squatters were not permanent settlers but moved with the frontier. They lived in crude Indian-style huts built of brush and small branches. Their food consisted almost entirely of wild game, and they even dressed like Indians in leather clothing with moccasins on their feet. If they stayed long enough in one place they might dig up a little ground to plant some Indian corn. They had no farm animals with them and often did not even have a family and certainly no wish to settle down as farmers. Such frontiersmen were common in colonial Pennsylvania and were always on the farthest line of the frontier.

Squire Boone was different. He was a farmer and in 1730 he bought about four hundred acres of land from the Penns. Boone's deed to his land describes him as a "yeoman," which in the language of the time meant that he was a farmer.

According to some accounts he had to cut down the trees on his land to clear it for farm use. These logs he used to build a two-story house in which Daniel was born. While building the house he lived in frontier fashion in a lean-to made from tree branches. Such a temporary home was essential while a man was building his permanent house and most pioneer farmers used such primitive dwellings.

Being a very active man Squire Boone was not content to be just a farmer, so he set up a blacksmith shop on his farm. Also, the Boones had been weavers in England and Squire was quick to see that a frontier settlement could use a skilled weaver. Pioneer farm women had much to do and spinning and weaving was a time-consuming task. The women could not always produce enough cloth for their large families. Boone's weaving business soon became a success, and not long after he started, he had five looms working. The children were put to work helping to run them.

Daniel's father seems to have prospered from this business, for not long after Daniel's birth Squire Boone began building a stone house. It is this stone house which the state of Pennsylvania acquired in 1937 and which has been carefully restored and furnished in the style of the time when Boone lived in it. A barn and blacksmith shop are also a part of the restored homestead. The state now owns the entire Boone farm and it is a historic shrine for American youth with a museum and a program to tell youth of today something about this great wilderness scout. A two-story log house built in 1732 in the nearby Oley Valley, similar to the one in which Boone was born, has been moved near the homestead and restored to its original condition.

The Boones must have lived a very busy life what with weaving, farming, and blacksmithing all going on at the same time. Boone's father and mother were too busy to keep a diary or write letters and really very little is recorded about their life in the Oley Valley. We know there wasn't

Soon after Daniel's birth, Squire Boone began to build this stone house, which has been carefully restored and furnished.

time for much schooling of the children and it is not even known whether there was a school in that still remote area. Boone's father once said, "Let the girls do the spellin' and Dan will do the shootin'." It seems clear that Dan did just that, and his lack of schooling is shown by the inscriptions he liked to carve on tree trunks where he hunted, such as "D Boone cilled a bar here."

Though Daniel's father did some farming and owned some cattle, it was the custom on the early frontier to hunt wild game to keep the table provided with meat. Every frontiersman had a gun and in the 1730s it was a short English-style musket. The Pennsylvania German gunsmiths in Lancaster County had not yet invented the famous Pennsylvania long rifle which came into use about twenty years later. So with his musket young Daniel roamed over the hills and learned how to live in the woods and how to creep up quietly on wild animals and shoot them to get meat for the family table. There were Indians about and young Boone must have met them and learned some of their ways and skills as hunters. Obviously he also learned something about blacksmithing at his father's smithy because he later was with the wagon train which supplied Braddock's army in western Pennsylvania in 1755.

Life in the Boone home must have been like that in every frontier home of that day. The Boones were a large family, which was common in those times when every child meant more help in the home, in the fields, or, as was the case with the Boones, at the loom. There were ten Boone children, the oldest of whom was Sarah, born in 1724, and the youngest was Hannah, born in 1746. Daniel had four sisters and five brothers and that may have been why Squire Boone started building a larger house soon after 1734.

In a little more than twenty years the Boones lived first in a rough shack, a log house, and then in a large stone house, which shows that the hardworking pioneer did not always live in poverty. The Boones probably had as good a life as anyone in this region, and the furnishings in the restored Boone Homestead, which are based on much study of how a house of this kind would have been furnished in the 1740s, give a good picture of the typical pioneer home of the time. It had a huge open fireplace for heating and cooking, and about it and from the mantel hung the necessary tin and iron cooking pots and pans of the early kitchen. The wooden furniture was rough and rugged enough to stand a lot of wear and tear. Almost all of it was made by

The kitchen of the Boone homestead is typical of others of that period. The food was cooked in the huge fireplace and served at the table nearby.

Squire Boone and his sons when long, dark winter days ended work out-of-doors. Philadelphia was the nearest town where furniture was made and sold and even if it had been available it would have been more expensive than a frontier family could afford.

It is easy to picture the Boone family gathered around the large kitchen table for an evening meal with perhaps a leg of venison from a deer young Daniel had killed. The vegetables, such as potatoes, turnips, squash, pumpkins and cabbage, were grown in the garden outside the house. The corn or wheat grown on the small farm was probably ground into meal and flour because grandfather Boone had a grist mill not far away. Home-baked wheat bread and corn bread, as well as cornmeal mush would have been on the Boones' table. Stew made from vegetables and meat was also a common dish. The food was certain to have been flavored mainly with herbs grown in the garden just outside the house. Sage, mustard, dill, rosemary, and fennel would have been among these herbs. After summer days were gone, the herbs were pulled up and hung from the kitchen rafters to dry, where they created a pleasing fragrance as well as serving as a handy herb store for the cook.

Life on the frontier was hard and the workday was from sunrise to dark. Occasionally after the evening meal home-made candles might be lighted, but only rarely because father, mother, and the children went to bed at an early hour. Sometimes on a winter evening the family sat around the blazing kitchen fire for storytelling and Dan may well have told his parents and brothers and sisters about the "bar" he shot on one of his hunting trips.

Another thing which made the Boones typical of the Pennsylvania frontier was Squire Boone's undying wanderlust. When Daniel was sixteen his father decided to move to the newly developing Yadkin River region in North Carolina. On May 1, 1750, the family packed all its belongings and began the long journey by horse and wagon down Pennsylvania's Cumberland Valley into Virginia's Shenandoah country, and on to North Carolina's Yadkin. What led Squire Boone to move is not known. He must have been prosperous in Pennsylvania, judging from his large stone house. Perhaps it was that the children had married outside the Quaker meeting and their father was finally disowned by the congregation for acting "contrary to discipline." In any case, he was following the American pioneer tradition rooted in Pennsylvania's frontier days.

At this time the frontier of settlement in Pennsylvania kept on pressing farther and farther westward even beyond the Allegheny Mountains. It was in western and northeastern Pennsylvania that a new frontier was created in the 1760s and 1770s before the Revolution. However, Connecticut claimed most of northern Pennsylvania and settlers from the Nutmeg State came into Pennsylvania's Wyoming Valley and were pioneers in creating a frontier in Wilkes-Barre and this region. The dispute between Pennsylvania and Connecticut was settled at last in favor of Pennsylvania, but the Connecticut settlers made a lasting imprint on the culture and life of the area.

The southwestern part of Pennsylvania was claimed by Virginia in a similar boundary dispute. The early charters were very vague and general so such conflicts were inevitable. It was not until after the Revolution that this disagreement with Virginia was settled and Pennsylvania again won.

It was of great importance that these arguments about boundaries were settled in favor of Pennsylvania because the state would have been very small indeed if Connecticut and Virginia had won control of the disputed areas. As it turned out Pennsylvania had enough land to allow her growing population to find satisfactory farms and homesteads.

chapter 7

George Washington and the French and Indian War in Pennsylvania

William Penn's dream of a Pennsylvania without war of any kind to interfere with growth and prosperity came to a rude end when England became involved early in the 1700s in a long series of wars with France which pulled her colonies into the action. Louis XIV of France had made his great palace in Versailles the center of power in Europe. England was a younger but ambitious nation which dared to challenge that power.

Only one of these wars involved Pennsylvania to any great extent and that was the last of them, which came to be known in North America as the French and Indian War. France had no active interest in Pennsylvania when the conflicts began with England, and if anyone had warned the Penns after their father's death that they should be on their guard against France, he would have been looked on with disbelief. Twenty years later, however, the threat from France was obvious.

It was all a matter of geography. A map of North America in 1720 clearly reveals the problem: France had two key centers of settlement there at that time. One was in what is now Canada around Montreal and Quebec, and the other was on the lower Mississippi River in what is now Louisiana. They were a long way from each other and France began to worry about this great distance when it made plans for protecting and expanding its North American empire. In the early days of French exploration in the New World, roving, adventuresome Frenchmen like Robert La Salle travelled all through the Mississippi and Ohio valleys and probably into what is now western Pennsylvania. As a result the French could claim western Pennsylvania by right of exploration before the English. This did not matter very much in the early days of Pennsylvania and it is not likely William Penn even knew about it.

New France, as the French empire in North America was known, began to grow and more settlers arrived, among them people interested in trade and commerce. The traders wanted beaver furs from the Indians in exchange for blankets, powder, guns, and trinkets. They learned about the Ohio and upper Mississippi River country and the rich fur trade in this region. English traders from Philadelphia had the same idea and by about 1730 they were starting to compete with the French in western Pennsylvania.

A more important source of conflict between the two countries was the desire of France to bring about more unity between its settlements in Canada and Louisiana. Paris had not paid much attention to New France before about 1730 and had not made any real effort to build a lasting empire in North America. When it did begin considering such a goal, the need to close the gap between eastern Canada and the lower Mississippi was clear. It led France for the first time to understand that western Pennsylvania was the key to doing this.

A map of the St. Lawrence River shows that ships can travel to and from the Great Lakes port of Erie in northwestern Pennsylvania. This was the basic route the French found over two hundred years ago in their search for a way to go primarily by water from Quebec and Montreal to the Ohio and Mississippi. Like other Europeans, the French knew next to nothing about North American geography. In 1739 and again ten years later they sent exploring expeditions down the St. Lawrence from Montreal, across southwestern New York and northwestern Pennsylvania by way of Lake Chautauqua to the Allegheny, then down to the Ohio, and on from there to the Mississippi. On the trip in 1749 they planted lead plates in the ground at key points laying claim to the land by France.

Early in the summer of 1752 a new and energetic governor of New France, the Marquis Duquesne, arrived with orders from his king to strengthen the claims of France in the Ohio region, which included northwestern Pennsylvania. After several months of preparation, early in 1753 an expedition of two thousand French soldiers and Indian allies began to move all the way from Montreal to what is now Erie. Large broad boats, which the French called *bateaux,* carried men and supplies down the St. Lawrence, into Lake Ontario, and then across Lake Erie. The earlier French explorers had reached western Pennsylvania at present-day Warren by way of Lake Chautauqua in New York, but by now the French had learned there was a good harbor at Erie and this was where they landed early in 1753. It was just a few miles eastward from there to what is today the sleepy little town of Waterford and here the French quickly moved men and supplies and built a small fort. It was named Fort Le Boeuf, and it protected tiny Le Boeuf Creek, which rises there and flows into French Creek, which in turn joins the Allegheny River at present-day Franklin. In this one move the French fortified the farthest headwaters of the Ohio. That same year they also built a fort at Erie named Fort Presque Isle to protect their landing and supply base. Later they erected forts at the junction of French Creek with the Allegheny at Franklin, and then moved farther down the Allegheny all the way to the head of the Ohio at present-day Pittsburgh. This last was called Fort Duquesne. All of these were small log forts built from trees cut down on the spot.

What was going on in this very remote western Pennsylvania wilderness was made known to London in remarkably short time for those days. London responded by telling her colonies to "repel force with force," but the Penns, who were now living in England, cared little and the Philadelphia Quakers were opposed to war, so Pennsylvania sat still. Virgina still claimed western Pennsylvania under its charter and did take an interest, especially because it had a very lively governor in Lord Dinwiddie and a few Virginians already had formed a land and trading company named the Ohio Company to sell land and to trade with the Indians in that region. The French were stepping on Virginia's toes and Virginia responded with action.

Governor Dinwiddie decided to send a mission through the wilderness to ask the French in a polite way to leave because they were on land claimed by England. At that time George Washington, just twenty-one, was a major in the Virginia militia, a surveyor and a landholder. Because of his work as a surveyor he was familiar with the western wilderness. Washington left Williamsburg on October 31, 1753, on horseback with his personal baggage, and was joined by a French interpreter at Fredericksburg and the scout Christopher Gist at Cumberland, Maryland, who knew the Indians and part of the country. It was a rough and dangerous journey full of perils beyond belief. When young Washington at last reached Fort Le Boeuf on December 11 to present his polite but strong request to the veteran

French commander Legardeur de St. Pierre, he was wined and dined but afterwards was politely told, "As to the summons you sent me to retire, I do not think myself obliged to obey it." Washington returned to Williamsburg on January 16, 1754, with this reply, after having dared death from drowning in crossing the Allegheny and shots from an Indian ambush, in a journey of several thousand miles through the wilderness.

Governor Dinwiddie saw the need for action and at once sent a small force of Virginia militia to build a fort at the forks of the Ohio which Washington had seen on his journey to Fort Le Boeuf and noted in his journal of the trip as "extremely well situated for a fort." For the English it was a case of too little and too late because they were hardly started on their fort early in 1754 when a strong French force arrived commanded by Sieur de Contrecoeur. On April 16 the Virginians were forced to surrender and the French started at once to build their own Fort Duquesne. Back at Williamsburg Washington had been promoted to lieutenant colonel by Governor Dinwiddie and ordered back to the forks of the Ohio with a larger force of men and supplies. Friendly Indians told him what had happened. Washington had to backtrack and built a temporary fort, which he aptly called Fort Necessity about twenty miles away, near present Uniontown. After several skirmishes, it became obvious that the French outnumbered the colonials so greatly that the colonials could not hope to win. Washington was forced to surrender on July 3, 1754. However, he and his men were allowed to march with their muskets out of the fort, now restored as part of a national historical park. Thus far the French and their Indian allies were in full control of western Pennsylvania.

When slow-moving ships finally arrived in London with this news there were those who said in effect, "This is not our war in this wilderness. Let those who went there as colonists fight and pay for it." But a larger number of Englishmen felt that it was their war since they considered the colonies essential to their empire. In January, 1755, the English sent General Edward Braddock, an experienced but pompous regular army officer, and about a thousand British veterans, to take on the French and Indians. They landed at Hampton Roads, Virginia, and Braddock started to move his army with all its supplies, wagons, and artillery toward Maryland. The Quaker Assembly at Philadelphia still refused to vote money for armed warfare but did provide for supplies which enabled Ben Franklin to buy a hundred and fifty big Conestoga wagons with four horses to each wagon, and fifteen hundred saddle or pack horses, loaded with supplies, which were assembled at Cumberland, Maryland.

Braddock, veteran of over forty years of warfare on European battlefronts, thought he knew everything about warfare and looked upon the colonial troops supposed to aid him as "very indifferent" soldiers. He told Washington, who came to lead the Virginia militia, that the French and Indians might be a terror to the colonial troops but they could hardly stand up to his Scotch Highlanders. Braddock knew so little about the task ahead of him that he actually believed he needed to march only about fifteen miles to reach Fort Duquesne. When he learned that the actual distance was more than a hundred miles through the wilderness, from his main supply base, he did not consider it a problem. He simply could not imagine the terrible difficulties of getting an army, heavy wagons, and cannon through the vast forested mountain country in western Maryland and Pennsylvania. In a line four miles long the British regulars marched in their bright red coats, colors flying, drums beating, and the fifes lustily playing the famous "Grenadiers March." Braddock, in full dress uniform, followed in his great coach. As they moved through the wilderness, Braddock began to think it was, as he put it,

"a drear and desolate" country. His army moved slowly
mile by rugged mile as the advancing axemen labored to
cut down trees and clear away saplings to make a rough
twelve-foot-wide path. It must have been a great sight for
the Indians who lurked in the forest on every side. They
kept the French at Fort Duquesne fully informed about
what this strange and even frightening army was doing, and
did not miss a chance to sink a tomahawk in the skull of any
straggler. Needless to say fear of this fate helped the officers
to keep the soldiers pretty much in the line of march.

By the afternoon of July 9, a force trimmed down at
Washington's suggestion to some twelve hundred men,
twelve cannon, thirty supply wagons, and the ammunition
train was within about six miles or one day's march of Fort
Duquesne and Braddock issued orders to select open ground
for a camp from which he would move on the fort the next
day. Braddock certainly must have been well satisfied with
his mission, for he had literally conquered a wilderness in
his three-month march from Fort Cumberland in Maryland. He would have been even more pleased had he known
how hopeless was the French cause. Fort Duquesne was not
very strongly held. Its commander, Captain Hyacinthe de
Beaujeu, had only about three hundred French soldiers
and Canadian militiamen within the small log fort, and
camped just outside a few hundred unreliable Indians. The
fort could have been blasted to bits by Braddock's cannon
in one round of firing. Beaujeu was so desperate he made
up his mind his only chance to survive was to march out
and attack the British before they got to him.

This led to one of the strangest battles in all the history
of North America. When Lieutenant Colonel Gage of the
British force moved ahead to select a camp site, he entered
a narrow path between two small wooded hills but did not
take the precaution of securing them against an enemy. It
was here that Captain Beaujeu led a wild head-on attack

on Gage. Beaujeu was shot down at once by the British soldiers who knelt and fired in ranks as they were taught to do. The French and Indians were scattered and the skirmish seemed to have been won by the British, but for some reason Gage failed to seize the advantage and drew back instead of advancing. The French second-in-command, Captain Jean Dumas, rallied his forces and ordered them to take to the woods and fire Indian style from behind trees and bushes upon the British veterans. A Pennsylvanian present, James Burd, wrote that "the Enemy kept behind trees and logs of Wood, and cut down our Troops" as fast as they could try to attack. Washington tried to get Braddock to abandon his British style of open fighting and to take to the protection of the woods frontier style, but the general stubbornly refused and shouted "cowards" at those of his men who tried to, striking them with the flat of his sword. There is no questioning Braddock's courage for four horses were shot from under him before he was mortally wounded mounting a fifth and carried on a litter from the carnage.

His wisdom, however, can be questioned. By four o'clock that afternoon he had lost at least half of his officers and men to a disorganized and much smaller force and with it the chance perhaps to have ended the French and Indian War. His reward was an unmarked grave in the western Pennsylvania wilderness, the exact location of which is not known. This was one of the saddest pages in British military history. Had Braddock heeded the advice of Washington and other colonial officers, victory could have been won by his larger force. The Indians were strong believers in the dictum that "he who fights and runs away may live to fight another day" and had the English also believed this, Captain Dumas could have been defeated. Washington later wrote his brother, "We have been most scandalously beaten by a trifling body of men." What was left of Braddock's army did not stop running until it reached Philadelphia.

The Indians, long awaiting a chance for revenge on the white settlers who had pushed them from their lands and hunting grounds, fell upon the frontier with savage glee, killing and scalping as they raided to within fifty miles of Philadelphia.

In faraway London a new and energetic prime minister named William Pitt came into power in 1757. He declared in effect that he was tired of France twisting the British lion's tail and that French power in North America must and should be broken. A new commander, Brig. Gen. John Forbes, and a new army of nearly eight thousand men was ordered to march on and capture Fort Duquesne. This new army landed at Philadelphia early in 1758. An entirely new route to the fort had been laid out by way of Carlisle and Raystown, now Bedford. Beyond Raystown, another but shorter road had to be cut through part of the wilderness. Forbes had become so ill he had to be carried on a litter but he had with him Colonel George Washington, his trusted advisor, and Colonel Henry Bouquet, a brilliant Swiss-born soldier, who quickly learned the art of frontier warfare. At Loyalhanna the British-colonial force built Fort Ligonier as a western base, and from here a smaller and lighter force advanced on Fort Duquesne, which they found to their surprise the French had abandoned and burned. The French had retreated when they learned that New France suffered defeat at Louisburg in Canada and on the high seas, which Britain's naval power now dominated. On November 25, 1758, General Forbes sat down at the ruins of the French fort and with his quill pen slowly scratched out a letter to William Pitt telling him of the victory and dating it from "Pittsburg." Immediately afterwards, he began building an English fort, the largest and strongest in North America, calling it Fort Pitt in honor of the prime minister. The Union Jack was now firmly planted at the forks of the Ohio and would fly there in serene splendor amid the wilderness

Braddock's defeat followed heavy open fighting during which he and over half his men courageously lost their lives.

until hauled down in the Revolution and replaced with the flag of the United States.

The French and Indian War did not really come to an end until the Treaty of Paris was signed in 1763 after the British won full control of Canada. In Pennsylvania, the French abandoned their forts all the way to Erie but the Indians continued the fight because they resented the defeat of their allies. New forts were built by the English at every site where the French had one, such as Franklin, Waterford, and Erie. Finally, in May, 1763, the Ohio Valley Indians, led by the fiery and able Pontiac, chief of the Ottawa, staged an all-out attack on the entire frontier from Detroit to Pittsburgh. By June they laid siege to powerful Fort Pitt and even attacked Fort Ligonier to the east.

Colonel Henry Bouquet was ordered by the British commander in chief, Lord Jeffrey Amherst, to march to the relief

of Fort Pitt with a battalion of the Royal Americans and two companies of Highlanders. Leaving Philadelphia in July, Bouquet moved some five hundred men with light supplies to Carlisle, on to Fort Bedford at Raystown, and by August 2 was at Fort Ligonier. There he left most of his wagons, had bags of flour loaded on pack horses, and moved even faster toward Fort Pitt only to run into a fierce ambush by the advancing Indians near the tiny stream of Bushy Run, close to present Greensburg and Jeanette. This was at about noon on August 5 and after several hours of bitter Indian-style fighting Bouquet got his men together on a "commodius piece of ground just spacious enough for our Purpose" and used the bags of flour to build a low bar-

The English were surprised to discover the ruins of Fort Duquesne, which the French had burned and abandoned.

ricade around his men. He had lost at least sixty men and some officers but from this hard-pressed waterless little camp "26 Miles from Fort Pitt," he sat down and calmly wrote to Lord Amherst describing what had happened, how brave had been his men as they "were attacked from every side, and the savages exerted themselves with uncommon resolution," and that "we expect to begin at daybreak." Though the letter was a calm and cool recital of the military situation, Bouquet ended with a confession of his doubts as to whether his embattled men could survive another day. Bouquet was attacked at the break of day, as he was able to write that night, by "shouting and yelling" Indians who moved in for the kill. The clever Swiss-born commander had learned much since he was with General Forbes and he refused to let the Indians pick their own way to fight. He gambled on dividing his force and sent a few of the Highlanders down the back of the hill as if they were retreating. The Indians rushed ahead with glee, but the Highlanders turned and attacked them from the rear. The gamble worked and the howling Indians attacking the camp soon found themselves blasted by the fire of the Highlanders at their rear.

Indians in warfare seldom were able to regroup their forces once their key plan of battle was upset as it now was at Bushy Run. They fled in disorder, and Bouquet, after resting his men overnight at Bushy Run and writing Amherst of his victory, was able to march the remaining twenty-six miles and reach Fort Pitt, where the Indians already had ended their siege. Pontiac's uprising was broken. The following year Colonel Bouquet marched farther into the Ohio country and for a time curbed the Indian menace. The days of frontier terror, when many a settler heard the fearsome warwhoop of marauding Indians, ended until the Revolution found the red man an ally of Great Britain and again on the warpath against the frontier settlers.

chapter 8

Ben Franklin's Philadelphia

No other colonial city excited the praise of European visitors as Philadelphia did. Peter Kalm, a Swedish visitor, wrote in 1747 that the city had "risen so suddenly from nothing into such grandeur and perfection" and that "its fine appearance, good regulations, agreeable location, natural advantages, trade, riches and power are by no means inferior to those of any, even the most ancient, towns in Europe." The English clergyman Andrew Burnaby, on the very first day of arriving wrote in 1759, "Philadelphia, if we consider that not eighty years ago the place where it now stands was a wild and uncultivated desert, inhabited by nothing but ravenous beasts, and a savage people, must certainly be the object of everyone's wonder and admiration." The well-planned streets, intersecting each other at right angles, and a "pavement of broad stones for foot passengers" along with "well lighted" streets at night "watched by a patrole" won his praise. What Burnaby called "the stadt house" was the Pennsylvania State House built to house the government of the colony, now known as Independence Hall, and Burnaby thought it "a large, handsome" building.

Since Europeans described Philadelphia in such glowing terms it is no wonder that colonials should become interested and even excited about this place, which by 1720 was already a small thriving city. Although he lived in Boston, Benjamin Franklin obviously read some of these reports and was impressed by them. Boston, which was the largest colonial city, did not hold much promise for him. The fifteenth child in a family of seventeen, young Ben at sixteen worked in a print shop owned by his older brother James. He washed, sorted, and set type for a newspaper, which he also printed on the heavy hand-operated press. In addition he delivered the papers every Thursday and at the same time took orders for ads and for printing jobs. In short, Ben did all the hard work while brother James raked in the profits. Ben began to think about escaping from this life of near slavery, and after saving money from his meager earnings he ran away and boarded a boat to New York. From there he walked across New Jersey, hitchhiked a boat ride down the Delaware, and arrived in Philadelphia on a bright, crisp Sunday morning in October to find the streets filled with "clean dressed" Quakers on their way to meeting. He was hungry but he had only a few copper cents in his wrinkled clothing. Happily he passed a bakery, where he bought three large penny rolls and started walking down Market Street. Years later he wrote in his *Autobiography* that a young girl laughed at him from a doorway on Market Street and that she was Deborah Read, who later became his wife. Something of what Franklin's Philadelphia looked like that autumn morning in 1723 still exists in Elfreths Alley, just off lower Market. It is a narrow street lined with eighteenth-century houses, some of which were there when Franklin came to the city.

The South East Prospect of The City of Philadelphia By Peter Cooper Painter

The Draw Bridge	7	John Witpain	13	Jo. Carpenter Store	19	Abr. Bickh.
2 Buds Building	8	Capt Anthony	14	Sam Carpenter Store	20	Thomas Masters
3 Edw Shipen	9	George Painter	15	S Carpenter Dock Hou	21	Sam. Perry
4 Ant Morris Brew Hou	10	Ios. Shipen	16	Sam Bunkley	22	Bank Meeting Hou
5 Capt Vineing	11	W Fisbearn Store	17	Quak Meeting Hou	23	Tho. Chalky
6 Ionethan Dickinson	12	The Scales	18	The Court Hou	24	Penny Pott Hou

The Philadelphia waterfront around 1720, as seen by folk art painter Peter Cooper.

Franklin immediately took to Philadelphia. This youngest colonial town was growing so fast it was on the way to being the largest. It was just the place for a bright, ambitious young man who seemed to have a new idea every day in a city ready to use one every day. The two had a love affair which never ended and made Franklin and Philadelphia the best-known features of colonial America. Young Franklin did what he knew how to do best, and that was printing. Before long he was official printer for the colony and even printed its new paper money.

Philadelphia's commerce was not unlike that of other ports except there was more of it and it was run by Quakers, whom everyone came to know as just about the shrewdest businessmen anywhere. Quakers and their Jewish friends ran just about every trading concern. These concerns were organized mostly as partnerships of two or three people. The start of most mercantile fortunes was in the Indian trade, but by 1750 wealth was to be found in trade with other colonies, the West Indies, and Europe. A few thousand English pounds, the equivalent of about a hundred thousand dollars in today's money, could start a merchant in business though the larger trading companies had perhaps ten times as much invested and traded directly with the West Indies and England. Philadelphia merchants sent goods by ship, often owned by themselves, and usually in charge was a young member of the firm who was learning the business.

Much of Philadelphia commerce was based on the famous triangular trade with the West Indies as the key. Peter Kalm wrote, "Philadelphia reaps the greatest profits from its trade to the West Indies, for thither the inhabitants ship almost every day a quantity of flour, butter, flesh and other victuals; timber, plank and the like. In return they receive either sugar, molasses, rum, indigo, mahogony and other goods, or ready money." He noted that "England supplies Philadelphia with almost all stuffs and manufactured goods which are wanted here." The produce of Pennsylvania sold in the West Indies was the source of the funds needed to buy manufactured goods from England and this was the triangle of trade.

In those days doing business was much more risky than it is today. Merchants had little idea what prices they would get for goods they shipped or had to pay for those they bought until they actually got to the place where they were sold and bought. This fluctuation in prices led to a lot of close bargaining and it was always a bit of a gamble whether a ship's cargo which started from Philadelphia to the West Indies would really produce a profit in Liverpool.

Philadelphia had wealth but those who had it were quiet and unassuming. The typical wealthy Quaker would not have his portrait painted because this was a show of vanity, but he might have a black-and-white crayon portrait drawn, which was more modest and also happened to be cheaper. He would own a nice carriage, and his clothing and that of his family would be plain but of very fine quality to mark him as no ordinary citizen. A rich Quaker lived on a higher social level but he remained somewhat puritanical. Although Quakers disapproved of the arts, which they thought had a taint of sin, they did ardently approve of learning and culture and supported these endeavors with their wealth. The earliest schools were started by Quakers, beginning with the Friends Public School in 1689. The Quakers had some new ideas on education, such as sending girls as well as boys to school and trying to give some practical training in vocations as well as the "three R's."

As Philadelphia grew, it was natural that many non-Quakers took part in the resulting prosperity. Indeed, by the time of the Revolution there were more non-Quakers than Quakers in the city that had been Penn's green country town. These people, of whom Ben Franklin was one, were not bound by Quaker austerity. Thus despite Quaker condemnation of the arts, other Philadelphians had the wealth and interest to aid the arts and culture. In Europe the arts were aided mostly by the kings and nobles, although all too often this support did not reflect any real interest. They helped an artist or a musician because it was the thing for kings and nobles to do. There was of course no noble class in Pennsylvania and the support of culture by a prosperous middle class showed the degree of their success and the growth of democracy. No person symbolized this better than Franklin.

He had not been in the Quaker city very long before his busy mind and his natural ability to make friends led him to organize his "ingenious acquaintances" in what he called the Junto, a word which comes from Spanish *junta* or "dis-

THE
Pennſylvania *GAZETTE*.

Containing the freſheſt Advices Foreign and Domeſtick.

From November 10. to November 17, 1737.

To the AUTHOR *of the* Pennſylvania
GAZETTE.

SIR,

 REEDOM OF SPEECH is a *principal Pillar* in a free Government: when this Support is taken away, the Conſtitution is diſſolved, and Tyranny is erected on its ruins. Republicks and limited Monarchies derive their ſtrength and vigour from a *Popular Examination* into the Actions of the Magiſtrates. This Privilege in all Ages has been and always will be abuſed. The beſt of Princes could not eſcape the cenſure and envy of the times they lived in. But the evil is not ſo great as it may appear at firſt Sight. A Magiſtrate, who ſincerely aims at the *Good* of the ſociety, will always have the inclinations of a great majority on his ſide; and impartial Poſterity will not fail to render him Juſtice.

These abuſes of the Freedom of Speech are the excreſcencies of Liberty. They ought to be ſuppreſſed; but to whom dare we commit the care of doing it? An evil Magiſtrate, entruſted with a **Power** to *puniſh Words*, is armed with a **Weapon** the moſt *deſtructive* and *terrible*. Under pretence of pruning off the exuberant branches, he frequently deſtroys the Tree.

It is certain, that he, who robs another of his moral reputation, more richly merits a Gibbet, than if he had plundered him of his purſe on the high-way. *Auguſtus Cæſar* under the ſpecious pretext of preſerving the characters of the *Romans* from defamation, introduced the Law, whereby *Libelling* was involved in the penalties of *Treaſon* againſt the State. This eſtabliſhed his Tyranny, and for one miſchief it prevented, ten thouſand evils, horrible and tremendous, ſprung up in the place. Thenceforward every perſon's life and fortune depended on the vile breath of Informers. The Conſtruction of words being arbitrary, and left to the deciſion of the Judges, no man could write or open his Mouth, without being in danger of forfeiting his Head.

One was put to death, for inſerting in his Hiſtory, the praiſes of *Brutus*; Another, for ſtiling *Caſſius* the *laſt* of the Romans. *Caligula* valued himſelf for being a notable Dancer; To deny He excelled in that manly accompliſhment was High-Treaſon. This Emperor advanced his Horſe *Incitatus* to the dignity of Conſul; and, tho' Hiſtory is ſilent, I don't queſtion but it was a capital crime to ſhow the leaſt contempt for that High Officer of State. Suppoſe then, any one had called the Prime Miniſter a *ſtupid animal.* The Emperor's Council might argue, that the malice of the Libel was aggravated by it's being true, and conſequently more likely to excite the family of this illuſtrious Magiſtrate to acts of revenge. Such a proſecution would appear ridiculous: Yet, if we may rely on Tra-

dition, there have been *formerly* Proconſuls in *America*, tho' of more malice, but hardly ſuperior in underſtanding to *Incitatus,* who would have thought themſelves *libelled*, to be called by their *proper names*.

Nero valued himſelf on his fine voice and ſkill in muſick; *a tandem ambition this!* He performed in public and carried the prize. It was afterwards Reſolved by all the Judges, as good Law, that whoever ſhould inſinuate the leaſt doubt of *Nero's* Pre-eminence in THE NOBLE ART OF FIDLING, ought to be deemed a Traitor to the State.

By the help of Inferences and Innuendo's, Treaſons multiplied in a prodigious manner. GRIEF was Treaſon. A Lady of noble birth was put to death for bewailing the loſs of her murdered Son. Silence was declared an overt act to prove the treaſonable purpoſes of the heart. LOOKS were conſtrued into Treaſon. *A ſerene open aſpect* was an evidence that the Perſon was pleaſed with the calamities that befel the Emperor. *A ſevere thoughtful countenance* was urged againſt the man that wore it, as a proof of his *plotting* againſt the State. DREAMS were often made capital offences. A new ſpecies of Informers went about *Rome*, inſinuating themſelves in all companies to fiſh out their Dreams, which the holy Prieſts, *O! nefarious wickedneſs!* interpreted into High-Treaſon. The *Romans* were ſo terrified by this ſtrange method of proceſs, that, far from diſcovering their Dreams, they durſt not own that they ſlept. In this terrible ſituation, when every one had ſo much cauſe to fear, even FEAR itſelf was made a *crime.* *Caligula* when he put his Brother to death, gave it as a reaſon to the Senate, that the Youth was afraid of being murdered. To be eminent in any virtue, either civil or military, was the greateſt crime a man could be guilty of. ------- *oh virtutes certiſſimum exitium.*

Theſe were ſome of the Effects of the Roman Law againſt Libelling.

THOSE of the Britiſh Kings who aimed at Deſpotic Power, or the oppreſſion of the Subject, conſtantly encouraged proſecutions for words.

Henry VII. a Prince mighty in politics, procured that Act to be paſſed, whereby the juriſdiction of the Star Chamber was confirmed and extended. Afterwards *Empſon* and *Dudley*, two voracious Dogs of prey, under the Protection of this High Court, exerciſed the moſt mercileſs acts of oppreſſion. The Subjects were terrified from uttering their griefs, while they ſaw the Thunder of the Star Chamber pointed at their Heads. This caution, however, could not prevent ſeveral dangerous tumults and inſurrections. For when the Tongues of the People are reſtrained, They commonly diſcharge their reſentments by a more *dangerous organ,* and break out into open acts of Violence.

During the Reign of *Henry* VIII. a high-ſpirited Monarch, every light expreſſion which happened to diſpleaſe him, was conſtrued by his ſouple Judges into a Libel, and ſometimes, extended to High-Treaſon. When Queen *Mary* of Bloody Memory, aſcended the Throne, the Parliament, in order to raiſe a *Fence* againſt the violent Proſecutions for Words, which had rendered the Lives, Liberties

The leading colonial newspaper was Benjamin Franklin's The Pennsylvania Gazette. This issue carried a long letter on political affairs.

cussion society." It was known by some as the Leather Apron Club because most members were workers and sometimes left their shops so hurriedly that they wore their aprons to the Friday evening discussion meetings. Typical of the ideas discussed was one Franklin once tossed out, "What is wisdom?" As a result of the discussions of the Junto, Franklin got the idea for the first library in America to circulate books, the Library Company of Philadelphia. This is a good example of Ben Franklin's imaginative thinking and also shows what young and vibrant Philadelphia could and did accept. Citizens could borrow books for a small fee and with the money the library bought more books from England. As Franklin put it, "Reading became quite fashionable."

Franklin's first love was his newspaper, *The Pennsylvania Gazette,* which became the leading newspaper of the colonies. He also quickly became famous for his yearly *Poor Richard's Almanack.* In his *Autobiography* he wrote that he wanted it to be a "proper vehicle for conveying instruction among the common people, who bought scarcely any other books; I therefore filled all the little spaces that occurred between the remarkable days of the calendar with proverbial sentences." These were such famous sayings that they are repeated even today such as "Little strokes fell great oaks," or "Early to bed and early to rise makes a man healthy, wealthy, and wise." The popularity of the *Almanack* spread not only throughout the colonies but also in Europe. Thus, it was not long before Franklin, and along with him, Philadelphia, were widely known.

The newspaper and almanac were not Franklin's only interests. His was a restless mind and he let it roam freely. It was Franklin who, with others, started the Pennsylvania Hospital in 1751, the first in the colonies. The Pennsylvania Academy, which he helped found, developed into the University of Pennsylvania. Near Independence Hall is the American Philosophical Society, the oldest society in Amer-

*The title page from
Poor Richard's Almanack
which, as its popularity
spread over Europe,
carried the fame of
Franklin and Philadelphia.*

ica founded to promote learning, literature, and science, one of Franklin's ideas. Everyone knows the story of Franklin's kite and how he proved lightning was electricity and invented the lightning rod to protect buildings. He also invented the Franklin stove in 1742, a cast-iron stove with doors connected to a chimney which heated a room more quickly than a fireplace—and the first real revolution in home heating since the fireplace itself. Bifocal glasses are credited to him. The list of Franklin's inventions is truly incredible.

What would Philadelphia have been like without Franklin? The answer is that it might not have been as great a center of culture and science as it was with him, but it probably would have been called the "Athens of America" even without him. Colonial Philadelphia had the wealth and the spirit of freedom which gave rise to a spirit of inquiry and acceptance of new ideas. While Franklin was the man best known in the colonies and abroad as a person of genuine culture and learning who was deeply interested in the new spirit of scientific inquiry, he was not the only such man in Philadelphia. Franklin was the leader in starting many things such as the Library Company, the Pennsylvania Hospital, and the American Philosophical Society, but other men worked with him. Dr. Thomas Bond and Dr. Benjamin Rush helped Franklin to found the Pennsylvania Hospital, and in 1763 they and others went on to open the first medical school at the College of Philadelphia.

David Rittenhouse of Philadelphia was a leader in the field of astronomy, making a first study of the transit of Venus. When he was about eighteen years old, he made what was probably the first telescope in America. In 1767 he designed and built an orrery, a device to record the movement of the planets. He invented and used instruments to survey land and to fix definite boundary lines. He built the first observatory in the colonies and his work was so well known he was elected to the Royal Astronomical Society in England. He followed Franklin as president of the American Philosophical Society.

James Logan, wealthy friend of William Penn and for a time the deputy governor of Pennsylvania, was interested in the study of plants and how they reproduced. He built up the finest scientific library in the colonies at his home, Stenton, still preserved in Philadelphia. Other scientists of note were Lewis Evans, who made the first accurate maps of Pennsylvania and the colonies; Thomas Godfrey, who invented the mariner's quadrant to aid in navigating the seas; and John Bartram, famous for his study of plants and plant life. Colonial Philadelphia was full of scientists and it is considered the birthplace of American science.

Philadelphians were wealthy enough by 1750 to begin to build some very fine homes and public buildings, and although there were few men who today would be called architects there were many able to copy the British Georgian style of architecture, and sometimes even to improve upon it. Named for the kings George of England, in whose reigns the style developed, this was architecture of great simplicity and grace. Quakers were not averse to building large homes when they became wealthy, and they liked the simple Georgian style. William Penn's Pennsbury was in Irish Georgian style. Many of the finest houses were built in what was then the Philadelphia countryside and the wealthy owners rode to their businesses in town in fine carriages. Though many of these houses have been destroyed as a result of modern growth, there are a number still standing in Fairmount Park and in Germantown. Among them are Stenton, Mt. Pleasant, Belmont, Cliveden, Hatfield House, Woodford, and Grumblethorp. Fine public buildings include the Pennsylvania Hospital's central building dating to the 1750s, Carpenters' Hall, and of course the Pennsylvania State House, which after 1824 became known as Independence Hall. Philadelphia is a nest of early American churches dating back to the 1700s which include the oldest, Gloria Dei (Old Swedes), Christ Church, St. Peter's, St. Mary's, and St. George's. It would take several days to visit and study all the colonial houses, churches, and public buildings which still remain in what may be called "Old Philadelphia." No other city can begin to equal it in fine old colonial buildings, landmarks of the past.

Another indication of Philadelphia's prosperity was the rising number of successful skilled craftsmen in business there. For even though a Quaker frowned on too much luxury, this did not mean that he would not buy a choice set of pewter or silver or some handsome Chippendale furniture for his home. And, of course, the wealthy who were not Quakers had no pangs of conscience about living well. Pewter, made from a mixture of about eighty percent tin and twenty percent lead or copper, was the most popular material for tableware, but before 1750 most of it was imported from England. The more expensive silver was also imported before that date, but by the Revolution Philadelphia was famous for its pewterers and silversmiths. Cesar Ghiselin and Philip Syng were noted silversmiths. "Baron" Stiegel's beautiful glassware, made at his glassworks at Manheim near Philadelphia, was known from Boston to Savannah even before 1776. Many a wealthy colonial in other seaboard cities learned that Philadelphia could provide crafted objects as fine or even finer than could be imported from England and at more modest prices. Tall clocks like

The Franklin stove, invented in 1742 by Ben himself, was the greatest innovation in heating since the fireplace.

those prized today as "grandfather clocks" were much in demand for household use and these also were a prized product of the skilled craftsmen of Philadelphia. The Philadelphia Museum of Art has many of these fine objects on display in its collections, as does the famous Winterthur Museum in Delaware.

In the arts Quaker austerity had a chilling but not killing effect because plenty of non-Quakers took an interest in one or other of the arts. The Germans had a deep love of music and the German immigrants who came to Philadelphia nurtured this love. They had a large part in founding the Orpheus Club in 1759, one of the first musical societies in the colonies. The first opera to be presented in Philadelphia was given that same year. It was also in 1759 that Francis Hopkinson composed "My Days Have Been so Wondrous Free," which could be called a "hit" of that day. For a time the theater had been almost nonexistent in colonial America because of the Puritans in New England and the hardly less severe Pennsylvania Quakers, but after 1750 it began to catch on even in Boston and Philadelphia. The Southwark Theater, one of the first in the colonies, was opened in Philadelphia in 1766 with *The Prince of Parthia,* by Thomas Godfrey, a Pennsylvania playwright. Because Quaker beliefs still carried great weight, it was sometimes necessary to dress up the play with titles that sounded very moral and proper, such as *The Fair Penitent.* Even Shakespeare's *Hamlet* was given the title of *Filial Piety.* Those who attended the theater had to put up with being unable to get reserved seats, lack of any heat, and often with hoodlums who hissed the actors and even threw apples or eggs at them. It took a hardy and adventurous actor to walk on a stage in early Philadelphia.

Philadelphia became a haven for early American artists, of whom the best known was Benjamin West. West was a Quaker born in 1738 in a house still standing in Swarthmore. His first painting was done when he was seven and it was a picture of his sister's sleeping baby, which he did secretly because he was afraid of what his mother would say. She is reported to have said, "Ben thee is not a good Quaker, but I like this." He began to paint birds and flowers and there is the well-known story of how he cut the hair from the tail of the family cat to make his first paint brushes. His artistic tendencies were brought up in the local Quaker meeting and some thought it was a sinful thing for him to do, but fortunately this did not stop him.

There was no one to teach West and no market for his work and he ended up in London as a youth, both to study and to paint. His paintings so pleased King George III that he was made a court artist. In his lifetime West painted more than four hundred pictures in his London studio. Among the most famous are *Penn's Treaty with the Indians* and *Christ Healing the Sick;* the latter done for the Pennsylvania Hospital. He was a founder of the Royal Academy of Art in London and while his great work was done in that country he aided many young American artists, of whom the best known is Charles Willson Peale, who studied under West but returned to Philadelphia to paint. By 1772 Peale had done his first of many portraits of Washington and his famous painting of the great general at Valley Forge. Gustavus Hesselius, an organ builder by trade, was an early Philadelphia artist noted for the portraits of two Delaware Indian chiefs that he did for Thomas Penn. Art was on the move and Franklin wrote about 1770 that "some of our young geniuses began to lisp attempts at painting, poetry, and music." Charles Willson Peale wrote that Philadelphians had "a growing taste for the arts, and are becoming more and more fond of encouraging their progress." By the time of the Revolution, Philadelphia was attracting attention for its painters, who after a time made it the art center of the new nation.

Colonial Virginia's Governor Berkeley is said to have once thanked God there were no printing presses in his colony. He would have been a very unhappy governor of Pennsylvania because printing flourished there. Of course Ben Franklin had a role in making Philadelphia what could be called a haven of the printing press. The first newspaper was started in 1719, the third in the colonies. The third newspaper in Philadelphia was Franklin's *Pennsylvania Gazette,* the first in the colonies to have an editorial column and cartoons. There were six newspapers in Philadelphia on the eve of the Revolution and the first American magazine had been published in 1741. Magazines had a hard time but were catching on by 1776. Newspapers in the German language were printed to meet the needs of the large German population.

Governor Berkeley did not like newspapers because he thought they encouraged dissent and new ideas which were not always agreeable to those in power. The number of newspapers in Pennsylvania helped more people to put their ideas on paper and at times they voiced dissent, but this is one reason Pennsylvania was a center for expressions of freedom in colonial times. In newspapers like the *Pennsylvania Gazette,* in printed pamphlets, and what were called broadsides, people argued the political ideas of the time. Franklin himself sometimes wrote unsigned articles just to stir up thinking about problems of the day. The inns and coffee houses of Philadelphia were full of hot discussion based on the newspapers. On the eve of the American Revolution it was the newspapers that presented the arguments for and against taxation without representation and what was thought to be the "tyranny" of England. It was a clear demonstration of belief in the idea that a free press is the sound foundation for government of a free people.

The painter of Staircase Group, *Charles Willson Peale, said Philadelphians had "a growing taste for the arts. . . ."*

These early newspapers were not much like those of today, for they were four pages of single-folded sheets about the size of a modern magazine. Most of the news was from England, but the French and Indian War and the doings of the provincial government were reported. The front page usually was made up of a long report on world events which, while they had happened abroad maybe months before, were fresh news in Philadelphia when received on the latest ship. News of the port was common, with names of ships coming and going and their cargo, and much of the remainder of the paper was taken up with small advertisements which today give a wonderful picture of early Philadelphia business—the kinds of merchandise for sale and the prices charged.

Philadelphia was not only the center of commerce and culture but it was also the center of colonial political affairs, and right in the middle of Pennsylvania politics after about 1750 was Benjamin Franklin. Past politics can be dull if described in too great detail so a few light strokes of the brush are enough in painting it. The Quakers were in complete control of the government of the province until the start of war with France. Under English law of the time, John Penn as the oldest son of William Penn inherited half of Pennsylvania, and his two brothers Thomas and Richard shared the other half. When John died in 1746, Thomas increased by inheritance his share to three-quarters and was governor of Pennsylvania until his death in 1775. Thomas had become an Anglican and seldom saw eye to eye with the Pennsylvania Quakers and so was quite unpopular. Quaker pacifism and the resulting unwillingness to fight to protect the frontier against the French and Indians weakened the Quakers' political strength as non-Quakers such as Franklin, and the Scotch-Irish and some Germans from the frontier counties began to get into politics.

From about 1750 to the Revolution there were two groups battling each other in Pennsylvania political affairs, one of

Benjamin Franklin came to be known as the leader of the common people.

which had the support of what might be called the common people and the other favoring the upper classes. Franklin became the leader of the common people, which led Thomas Penn to call him "a dangerous man," and "sort of tribune of the people." Franklin probably liked that. Under Franklin's guidance, a system of volunteers called the Associators was set up to defend the province in the French and Indian War. This group was the ancestor of today's National Guard. Franklin helped also to raise supplies such as food, wagons, and horses for the English forces. He took the lead in getting the Assembly to build forts to protect the frontier after Braddock's defeat. Through all this period there was a growing demand for more democracy in the government and more representation in the Assembly from the new western counties and the common people in Philadelphia. Out of this conflict grew a spirit of independence which finally led to the American Revolution.

chapter 9

Life in Town and Country

While Philadelphia was growing and becoming a center of trade and culture, changes were also taking place in other parts of Pennsylvania. Towns were growing up throughout the colony and these interior towns were copies of the larger and richer capital. Reading, Lancaster, and York were started much as Philadelphia had started. They were the seats of the county and local government where court was held and the other business of government was carried on. This alone made them important and they were bound to grow.

None of them were cities as measured by today's standards but they were really small cities for that time, with all the types of activity and the life that went on in Philadelphia. They were what one historian has called "cities in the wilderness." Lancaster, founded in 1730, was the largest such town and by 1750 it had two thousand people and in 1775 about three thousand. At the start of the Revolution,

York was a town of seventeen hundred and Reading was a little larger. Small though they were, these towns were keys to the interior. They were laid out at vantage points for trade and travel. Reading was on the Schuylkill River and Lancaster and York were on the old Indian paths to the west.

As the interior towns grew they built the best schools and the largest churches. Before the Revolution, Lancaster built a church larger than any in Philadelphia. In the county seats the newly built courthouse took the place of Philadelphia's State House and around it was centered much of the town's business life. Since these towns were laid out by order of the Penns they resembled Philadelphia in their regular pattern of streets and somewhat modest two-story houses. Even the same street names, such as Locust, Chestnut, and Walnut, were not uncommon.

The town became the key to trade and commerce in the interior in much the same way as did Philadelphia as a port with foreign markets. Here were the merchants and their stores which took the produce of the farmer in exchange for what were usually in those days called "store goods" imported from Philadelphia and brought in by pack team or wagons. Cloth, hardware, spices, tea, and other luxury goods were among these. Back to Philadelphia went the farm produce in exchange for the "store goods." Much of this type of early trade was carried on without actual use of money because money was scarce in any new settlement and an exchange or barter system was used. It may have been a very crude system, as we think of business today, but it worked and it helped Pennsylvania grow in wealth. Pennsylvania in time had a paper money known as Pennsylvania currency but the gold or silver coins were either English coins or Spanish pieces of eight.

Obviously, these towns needed to be linked by either waterways or roads with the port of Philadelphia. Since most of the early growth of settlement was directly west from Philadelphia, an area that contained no waterways, roads became very important. Westward from Philadelphia ran one of the most heavily traveled Indian paths in the province known as the Great Minquas Path. It extended from the Delaware to a Susquehannock Indian fort on the Susquehanna below present Columbia. Very early traders on horseback with their goods on pack horses had used this path. And the most important road opening up trade to and from Philadelphia was the famous Conestoga Road to Lancaster which followed the Minquas Path almost to the Susquehanna and then turned northward to the new town of Lancaster. Lancaster people asked for it as early as 1731 to get their goods to market. It was finished in 1733 and made possible for the first time direct carrying of goods by wagon to and from Philadelphia and Lancaster.

It must not be thought that what was called a road at this time was anything like a hard-surfaced or even a good dirt or gravel road of later date. Building a road in colonial times meant surveying a route, cutting down trees where necessary, pulling out the larger stumps, and smoothing as best could be done a rough roadway about twelve feet wide. Early road builders were even a little careless about removing the stumps.

The resulting need for a heavy freight wagon which could move over the muddy, deeply rutted, unpaved road led to the invention of the famous Conestoga wagon, a heavy oak-framed wagon with wide wooden wheels covered with wide iron tires. The small and lightly built English wagons known to the earliest settlers were not built for this type of travel and Pennsylvania wagon makers and blacksmiths began to develop the Conestoga wagon, so called because one of the first places where it was built and used was in the narrow valley of Conestoga Creek in Lancaster County. By 1740 they were in use on the road to Philadelphia.

The first wagoners were mainly farmers willing to haul

goods in their wagons when they could not work on the farm. One observer wrote in 1753, "Every German farmer in our Province, almost, has a Waggon of his own." Companies later were organized which carried freight as a business. Stage lines ran a few passenger coaches between Philadelphia and nearby towns. One went as far as New York from Philadelphia by 1732 but the journey took a week. By 1771 a better coach service was advertised: it took only two days and the new stage was excitingly termed "The Flying Machine."

There were three classes of people in the social structure of the town. The merchant was at the very top because of his wealth. Some merchants, like Joseph Simon of Lancaster

"Every German farmer in our Province, almost, has a Waggon of his own." The Conestoga wagon had its origin in the valley of Conestoga Creek in Lancaster County.

with his great trading house, were among the wealthiest men in colonial America and today would be rated as millionaires. The top officials in the county government and leading lawyers and doctors also were part of this upper class. The middle class was made up of lesser merchants who owned what were called country stores, lawyers who had not yet become prominent, the keepers of shops, and craftsmen. Common laborers and servants who worked for wages were the lower class, but below them was the indentured or bound servant, owned for a number of years by the person for whom he or she worked, and then Negro slaves at the bottom. This class structure resembled that of England except that there was no nobility. The colonial upper class tried hard to copy the manners and ways of living of the English upper class.

The most important difference between the English social structure and that of colonial Pennsylvania was the ease with which those in a lower class in the colony could with a little luck and good fortune move into a higher class. Land was cheap and wages were good so that a person who followed Franklin's "a penny saved is a penny earned" philosophy could indeed better his lot in life. This mobility was the foundation of the concept of equality on which America has so prided itself.

The marked differences in the way these social classes lived made it possible for any observer quickly to tell an aristocrat from a common citizen. One mark of distinction was the house in which a man lived. The wealthy merchant lived in a fine Georgian-style house of stone or brick copied from houses in Philadelphia. The houses of the middle class were smaller, often two-story log buildings, or possibly less elegant stone houses. The lower class or commoners lived usually in what was little more than a log cabin or at best a tiny stone house. Furnishings in these homes also varied with the wealth of the owners. As prosperity increased, other marks of the aristocrat were servants and a fine carriage. In the middle class the women did their own house-work and the family rode in a light buggy. Below the middle class, people walked or rode horseback. Of course, travel conditions and roads being what they were, many an aristocrat sometimes also rode horseback.

Dress was a significant indication of class in those days. The colonial gentleman and his lady copied the finest styles of Paris and London. The men wore fancy bright velvet or satin waistcoats with gold buttons over white shirts of silk or linen with ruffled lace front and sleeves. Equally colorful velvet breeches reached to the knee and were worn over white silk stockings. Square-toed shoes were ornamented with silver buckles. Every gentleman wore a fancy wig pow-dered and curled so nicely that it needed weekly care by a barber who cleaned it and if necessary set the curls. The hat was a cocked three-cornered type decorated with gold braid.

In early Pennsylvania the Quaker men avoided the bright colors, fancy frills, and lace common to the dress of the grand gentlemen. They dressed in the same basic style but tended to drab browns or grays, avoided lace, and wore plain shoes without buckles. The proper Quaker also wore his hat with a plain flat brim. As time went on the wealthy Quaker merchant copied the more colorful fashions of the time.

The dress of the lady of the time was as distinctive and colorful. Fashionable dresses were made from luxurious fabrics such as brocades and velvets, decorated with trim-mings and lace. One style imported from Paris hung straight from the shoulders over petticoats fashioned around the large hoops common to women's dress of the time and reached to the ankles. Another popular style was the low-cut bodice or blouse with short sleeves heavily trimmed with lace. A floor-length outer skirt was lifted and looped back to show billowing petticoats of brilliantly colored silk which ballooned out over the huge hoops as much as four feet in width. Indeed, skirts were so wide that it was hard to seat two ladies together in a coach and a special chair with cut-off arms was cleverly designed by carriage builders to take care of this. The ladies wore their hair piled high on the head in a fashion resembling a small tower, which was carefully powdered and curled. Many ladies are said to have used a wooden block as a pillow in order to protect these hair-dos. Since it was impossible to wear a hat over such a hair style, ladies wore instead a small cap of lace. A tiny high-heel shoe (most women of that time had very small feet), sometimes decorated with a small silver buckle, went with a lady's fancy dress. Of course, the upper classes did not dress in such an elaborate way all the time. The extent to which the gentleman and his lady changed society dress for that of every day varied with the ideas of the person and the tasks involved. The basic style of dress did not vary but men and women were dressed in less finery while taking care of business or household chores.

The dress of the middle class and the common people is less well known. They are rarely pictured in the portraits of the times for the simple reason they could not afford portraits. There is no doubt the middle class copied the styles of the aristocracy in less ornate and cheaper versions. In his shop the craftsman wore a linen shirt and knee breeches of coarse cloth, and usually a leather apron. He also wore coarse cotton stockings and heavy, sturdy shoes. The ordinary laborer dressed in a general style similar to the craftsman but with coarser material used in clothing. Because they were usually working people, the commoner's wife and the female servant wore a loose and flowing garment as a dress over their undergarments.

The lot of the laborer was not a hard one in a Pennsylvania town. An early visitor noticed that "If a workman will work only four or five days in a week, he can live grandly." An ordinary workman could earn what in today's money would be several dollars a month with what was called "keep," which meant food and lodging. Women house servants earned about half as much, but an unskilled iron worker could earn twice as much.

The shortage of labor which could be hired for wages was the main reason why early Pennsylvania used many workers who were indentured servants, or redemptioners, who sold their services to redeem the cost of their coming on ship. The period of service was approximately five years. What were called "bound servants," people bound out for work by the courts, were common in early Pennsylvania. Servants of all kinds generally were well treated, partly because they were hard to get and also because there were laws to protect them against abuse. The province required they be given some tools, clothing, or money when released and it also gave redemptioners fifty acres of land.

Negro slavery was legal in colonial Pennsylvania and at the time of the Revolution approximately a fifth of the population was Negro. Even William Penn had a few slaves, though the Quaker religion was not in favor of slavery. It is hard to understand why Penn would have put up with it. The first opposition to slavery in America was made known by the Germantown Quaker-Mennonite community in 1688. There is every reason to believe that Quaker ship-owners, despite their religious beliefs, helped bring slaves to America.

The colonial town was not a very elegant place if looked at in today's terms. It had no water supply other than the home well and the town pump, and sanitary facilities even for the wealthy consisted of the outdoor toilet or outhouse. Streets were dirt roads that became muddy in winter or when it rained, and dusty in summer. There were no sidewalks or lights. Men wore high boots when walking and it was not uncommon for ladies to take off their shoes and carry them in hand because of the mud.

But while such a life may appear very uncomfortable to us, the past is only to be understood in terms of the standards of the time. The diaries and letters which remain and the news items in the few early colonial newspapers do not paint a picture of hardship or distress as the colonial towns-man looked at it. There were dances and parties as well as visits between friends. The local tavern and private clubs common in and out of Philadelphia helped add zest at least to the life of men. Going to church on Sunday was a major event for the family of that time, and everyone got out the "Sunday best" in clothing and carriage to meet and talk with other people. Weddings and even funerals also brought people together. Families were large and since there were few outside distractions family life was closer knit than today. In Pennsylvania today Amish young men may be seen on Sunday afternoon in a horse and buggy with their "best girl" on a "courting" drive and the same thing certainly went on two hundred years ago in the towns of the same region and in the surrounding countryside.

There was not much leisure in the life of the townsman of colonial times and no matter how wealthy the merchant, he was kept busy from early morning until dusk at his store or trading post. The streets of the early Pennsylvania town were lined with small shops in which the craftsmen were at work and they too were busy from early in the day until the lack of light made further work impossible. The smoky flickering candle was the only lighting in home or shop, which is another reason why there was little colonial night life.

It must have been quite an adventure for a child from an upper-class home in a colonial Pennsylvania town to have visited the cobbler's shop. His foot was placed on a piece of leather and the cobbler traced its outline and then matched it with a last, a foot-shaped form. There was only one for each size because shoes were made to fit either foot. On the same journey a potter's shop might be visited where mother could look for dishes which the potter turned from clay on a wheel run by a foot treadle. They might also go to the joiner's shop run by a man who made furniture on order or mended that which was broken. If it were a wealthy family riding in a carriage, a stop might be made at the blacksmith's shop to see whether the horse's shoes were on tightly. In Lancaster by the time of the Revolution there would have been a tailor shop where the gentleman, his lady, and children could have clothing made. There might even be a stop at the wig shop to leave father's wig which needed cleaning and curling or to pick up one that had been left on an earlier trip. A visit to such shops may be made at the William Penn Memorial Museum and more extensively at the Pennsylvania Farm Museum which re-create this way of life and show shops of an early day.

Not much is known about the life of children in colonial days. The dress of the children of the wealthy was a smaller-sized version of those their elders wore and must have been quite uncomfortable. Boys wore a waistcoat, knee breeches, stockings, and shoes much like their father's, and girls wore the flaring skirts fashionable for their mothers. Children of the lower classes dressed more comfortably out of necessity but even so boys dressed in coat and knee breeches and girls in long dresses, but these were made from a coarser cloth and with less frills than common to children of the well-to-do.

Colonial education was backward mainly because children, except for the wealthy, had so much work to do that there was little time for learning. The best schools of the time were located in the towns. But these were not free public schools and were attended only by those whose parents were able to pay for education. The most elementary work in reading, writing, and simple arithmetic was all even the best schools taught and both pupils and teachers were males. Sometimes the wealthy hired private tutors to educate their sons. With few exceptions, girls were very much neglected in the education of the time, and it is said that the wives of some leading patriots of the Revolution were not able to read or write.

The sons of wealthy merchants and craftsmen were apt to be trained in their father's work, and the children of laborers or servants were almost certain to take up the same livelihood. Girls who had the good fortune to be born into a home of wealth were taught to be "ladies," which meant instruction in the art of fine manners and dress and little else. Those born into a lower class fitted into the life of the family with little future other than that of aspiring to marrying a likely young man. It was a day in which children were best "seen and not heard," and family discipline was certain to be severe.

In colonial days Pennsylvanians were very religious and the church played a large part in their lives. Every community had its churches and going to church in "Sunday best" clothing was a great occasion in either town or country. It has been said that the "groves were God's first temples" because sometimes early religious services were held in a clearing in the woods by travelling ministers who moved from settlement to settlement. Often, before churches were built, services were held in homes. In towns and country communities, the first church was apt to be built of logs, but soon stone or brick buildings became common. Sermons of the day were long and full of threats of the horrible fate that could come to the sinner who did not repent of his or her evil ways. The Amish, Quakers, and Mennonites of course had a more simple way of worship and did not practice "hell fire and damnation" sermons but used a simple, quiet service of worship.

Country life in colonial Pennsylvania varied from life on the farthest frontier to life on the prosperous farms of Pennsylvania countryside which had been settled long before the Revolution. Although there were some similarities in these two kinds of country life, for the most part they were quite different. Visitors to early Pennsylvania wrote about the prosperity of the German farms in southeastern Pennsylvania and especially about their fine barns. Indeed, some thought the barns were nicer than the houses. At least two-thirds of the German immigrants were farmers and by 1750 there were about 90,000 of them out of a total of 190,000 people in the colony. As early as 1747 Governor George Thomas wrote, "The Germans of Pennsylvania . . . have by their industry been the principle [*sic*] implement of raising the state to its present flourishing condition, beyond any of His Majesty's colonies in North America." A French visitor several years later said, "The Germans are regarded as the most honest, most industrious and most economical of farmers." They made the limestone country of central Pennsylvania blossom, and it was soon known as the "bread-basket of America" because of its flourishing fields of wheat.

Frontier farmers had to cut their farms out of the wilderness by clearing the land of trees, but this hard task was over in the settled regions by midcentury. Also, on the frontier the farmer had to hunt wild game to supply meat for the family table but that day had ended for the settled farmer. Farm animals and the farmer's garden and fruit orchards furnished food. In the most settled parts of Pennsylvania those who lived on a farm in colonial times lived almost completely on the products of the farm and, other than flour or meal, very little was needed from outside. The houses in which country people lived began to improve in the older parts of the colony. A farmer often started life in a log cabin, as did Daniel Boone's father near Reading, but it was not long before at least a two-story log house was built and often a stone house. There was an old German saying, "A son should always begin his improvements where his father left off," and this often meant that the son built a stone house to replace the old log house. Very little brick was used in the German country. A traveller named Thomas Anbury in 1778 noticed that in Lancaster County, "Some of the farm houses are built of stone, two stories high and covered with cedar shingles." He went on to say, "The farmers of Pennsylvania pay more attention to the construction of their barns than their dwelling houses."

Life even on the well-established farms of the time was not easy, in spite of greater prosperity. Farm implements did not change much in those days. Grain was cut with a wooden cradle and stored in the barn to dry. When it was dry the sturdy farmer and his sons had to thresh or beat the grain out of the husks with a flail, two long sticks of wood tied together with a strip of leather. One of these sticks was held and the other was allowed to swing free and hit the piles of grain. This was hard work, demanding a strong back and lots of muscle in the arms. A prosperous farmer had a wagon by 1750, two or three smaller carts, and sleds and sleighs for winter use. Until heavier wagons came into use and roads were built on which they could be used, the plodding oxen were the common beasts of burden. Few early farms had horses and not many cattle were raised in colonial days. There were usually pigs and a few sheep to provide wool.

Life in the farm home did not change much either. It certainly must have been more comfortable to live in a two-story house than in a one-room cabin, but the kitchen with its fireplace in which were hung the pots and pans used in cooking remained the most important room. It was also the dining room because it was close to the place where the food was prepared. Until Franklin invented his cast-iron stove, the fireplace was the only method of heating houses large or small. But the Franklin stove was expensive and most farm homes had only the kitchen fireplace for warmth. The bedrooms upstairs often were not heated at all. Of course, the mansions of the wealthy had a fireplace in every room.

Houses had a central hall running from front to back and on one side was the living room with its tables and chairs and spinning wheel. On the other side was what was early called the "best room" or parlor where visitors were entertained and the family might sit on a Sunday afternoon. The attic was used to store things and the cellar was the place where apples, meat, and potatoes were kept. More prosperous farmers had a small building outside used for smoking meats and sometimes an outdoor baking oven. Furniture and household utensils, except for the pots and pans for cooking, were still made at home from wood. There were no carpets in colonial times and the hardwood floors were kept neatly polished. Farm families were large and the old adage that "many hands make light work" applied. The sons worked in the fields and helped out with the winter work of making tools and furniture, and the daughters helped their mother with housework and the spinning and weaving.

The farm family was clothed with rough cloth known as linsey-woolsey because it was a mixture of linen and wool, spun and woven at home. A cloth woven without wool was called "tow." The farmer wore shirt or jackets and breeches. Farm women wore ankle-length gowns and petticoats of linsey-woolsey in summer and pure wool in winter with a sunbonnet for summer sun and hood or shawl for winter's blasts. The children on a farm were dressed in smaller versions of the adult clothing. Nearly every early settler had a few fine garments brought from the old country and kept for "best," which meant some very special occasion such as a wedding or funeral. The first cloth to challenge homespun was calico which began to appear on the shelves of country stores and town shops, and some farm housewives owned fine calico dresses by the time of Revolution.

Colonial Pennsylvanians, whether living in town or country, were hearty eaters, and it is hard to believe reports of the variety and amount of food that was served at a single meal. The Germans especially loved to eat. Pennsylvania German country is still famous for the ample meals set on the family table. Pork, beef, and poultry were the principal meats served, and often all were served at the same meal. The Germans were great lovers of bread and huge quantities of it were baked at home. An early observer of Pennsylvania country life wrote, "The homes of the more prosperous farmers were provisioned as to stand a siege." There were all kinds of cured and smoked meats, fruits, vegetables, preserves and pickles, dried onions and herbs, apple butter, cider, and so on in the family larder in town and country and to these were often added venison and possibly even bear or wild turkey, grouse, and squirrels from the nearby woods. Someone has said that "not bread but meat was the staff of life" for most Pennsylvanians. Every home, whether in the town or on a farm, had a large garden in which vegetables were grown, along with aromatic herbs used in cooking. This abundance of food was probably a reason for Pennsylvania meals which a New England Yankee once called "a most sinful feast."

The stern and hard life of the colonial farmer was lightened by what was called "neighboring." Visiting between families was common and at such times the elders talked about crops, probably politics, and neighborhood gossip while the children played games before the fireplace. Farmers often exchanged work and several farmers joined in helping one another plant or harvest. Neighboring farmers also got together in what were called frolics or bees to help each other in building a cabin or to "raise" a house or possibly a community church or school house. Farm people who lived near Philadelphia or the larger towns were frequent visitors there, primarily to attend the markets held on the town squares at least once a week. Here the farmers displayed their produce for sale and also undoubtedly did some shopping and possibly dropped in at the town tavern for a little idle gossip with friends.

The Pennsylvania Germans, being great lovers of music, made use of the first church organs built in America. Church

Part of the Seventh-Day Baptist settlement at Ephrata. These buildings once rang with some of the first original expressions of American music.

services were enlivened by the lusty singing of hymns. The choral and instrumental music of the Moravians at Bethlehem and the male and female chorus at the Ephrata monastery of the Seventh-Day Baptists were the first original expressions of American music. The settlers brought with them many folk songs from the old country and these were often sung in the firelight of the farm and town home. The Moravians even set up a "Collegium Musicum" to train musicians and give concerts. Washington and others are said to have travelled long distances to hear the Moravian music.

Apart from visiting, weddings, and the like, there were not many kinds of amusement in early Pennsylvania.

Quaker-dominated early Pennsylvania did not start out to be exactly a place of joy. The Great Law in 1682 listed as "offenses against God" such things as "prizes, stage plays, cards, dice, May-games, masques, revels, bull-baiting, cock-fighting, and the like" saying that any or all of these could "excite the people to rudeness, cruelty and irreligion." They were "enticing, vain, and evil sports and practices" which were subject to a fine of five shillings or five days in jail at hard labor. Any work or play on Sunday was sinful and illegal. Early court records show these severe laws were often enforced, and people were brought into court for breaking them. Bullbaiting and cockfighting are looked upon today as barbaric amusements, but of course cards, plays, and games are another matter. However, it is hard to curb the natural instincts of people by law, and so colonial Pennsylvania was not a place entirely without fun. Quakers and members of such German sects as the Amish and Mennonites followed a strict life but others certainly managed to enjoy themselves more than might be thought. People got together for occasional dances, for singing, and for card playing.

Sitting in comfortable homes with every household convenience and radio and television at hand and one or two cars in the garage ready to take anyone, father, mother, or children just about anywhere over fine roads, we must think of colonial life as rough and drab, certainly not very exciting, if not downright uncomfortable. But if we look at it in terms of the life of the times, from Pennsylvania's founding to the American Revolution, we can see that it was changing for the better all of the time. People were becoming more prosperous and improving their way of life from that lived by earliest pioneers. Using a little imagination we can get a glimpse of people who had their trials and troubles common to their time but who for the most part lived contented and even happy lives.

chapter 10

All Men Are Created Equal

Men from Pennsylvania had leading roles in the events which finally led to outright revolt against England. When things settled down after the defeat of France in the French and Indian War, England found herself with an enormous national debt. The series of wars against France had cost a great deal of money. In addition, as the result of her victory England had won all of Canada, India, and much of the West Indies. In order to keep control of these territories, the English had to maintain expensive governmental offices and garrisons of soldiers in all of these countries. Thus, England was desperately in need of money, and it seemed only natural to the king and Parliament to seek at least part of this money by taxing the flourishing colonies in North America, which England had fought to protect. However, what seemed natural on the English side of the Atlantic seemed oppressive and arbitrary on the colonial side.

In 1765 Parliament passed the Stamp Act, which made it

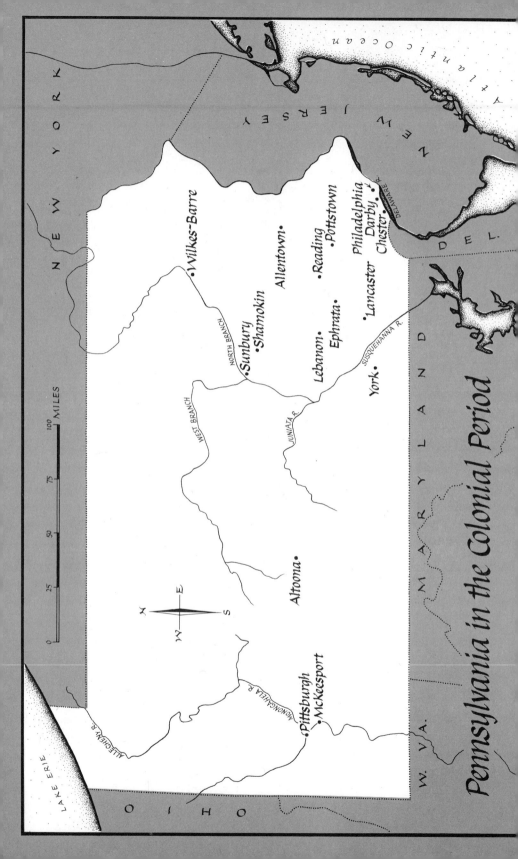

Pennsylvania in the Colonial Period

NEW YORK

NEW JERSEY

Atlantic Ocean

DEL.

MARYLAND

W. VA.

OHIO

LAKE ERIE

MILES

0   25   50   75   100

N
W   E
S

•Wilkes-Barre

NORTH BRANCH

•Sunbury
•Shamokin

Allentown•

•Reading
•Pottstown

Philadelphia
Darby
Chester•

DELAWARE R.

Lebanon•
Ephrata•

•Lancaster

York•

SUSQUEHANNA R.

WEST BRANCH

JUNIATA R.

Altoona•

•Pittsburgh
•McKeesport

MONONGAHELA R.

ALLEGHENY R.

necessary for colonists to buy a tax stamp for newspapers, legal documents, licenses, and even playing cards. Such a tax had been in effect in England, and the law applying it to the colonies said the money raised would be used for "defraying the necessary expenses of defending, protecting, and securing, the . . . colonies." It met at once with violent opposition in the colonies. Benjamin Franklin, who was in London at this time, considered it was a proper tax and made himself so unpopular in saying so that Deborah Franklin barricaded their house in Philadelphia against a possible mob. Franklin had been in London off and on since 1757 as a governmental agent of Pennsylvania. When it became clear to Parliament how strong colonial resistance to the act was, the House of Commons considered repeal and called Franklin to testify. By now Franklin realized why the colonies were opposed, and he had changed his own position. In order to make clear the colonists' grievances, Franklin had friends in the House ask him two questions. "What used to be the pride of America?" was the first, and to it he answered, "To indulge in the fashions and manufactures of Great Britain." The second was, "What is now their pride?" to which he answered, "To wear their old clothes over again, till they can make new ones." Franklin's forceful presentation of the colonial position was convincing and helped bring about the repeal of the tax.

John Dickinson, another Pennsylvania leader, came to the fore in the crisis over the Stamp Act. A Stamp Act Congress met in New York in October, 1765, and Dickinson, who represented Pennsylvania, wrote much of the Declaration of Rights and Petition to the King adopted by the meeting. These documents argued that the colonies must have the right to levy their own taxes since they were not represented in Parliament. When Great Britain replaced the stamp tax with others, such as the famous tax on tea, Dickinson took pen in hand and wrote the *Letters from a*

Farmer in Pennsylvania, which declared the taxes were an attack on liberty. Dickinson still thought of himself as a loyal British subject and wrote, "Let us behave like dutiful children, who have received unmerited blows from a beloved parent."

What prompted this strong feeling of protest on the part of the Pennsylvanians and the other colonists? One answer is that they were beginning to feel a sense of unity growing out of their efforts at common action during the colonial wars, which had started with King William's War in 1689 and lasted through Queen Anne's War, ended in 1713, and King George's War, ended in 1748. Franklin himself had helped create this thinking. In 1751 he wrote an essay titled "Observations Concerning the Increase of Mankind, Peopling of Countries, & c.," which painted a glowing picture of the destiny of America and of the British Empire in populating lands to the west. Franklin did say that the colonies should be free to handle their own internal problems. In 1754 he was in Albany, New York, and at a meeting of men from seven of the colonies Franklin set forth the Albany Plan for Union, which would have unified the colonies in several actions, such as common defense and settling western lands. It was a bold plan, and Franklin always believed it could have prevented the Revolution by creating a colonial government that could work in harmony with the mother country. The colonies turned it down. "But," as Franklin later said, "history is full of the errors of states and princes. . . ." This sense of unity was increased by the French and Indian War as colonial soldiers from Pennsylvania, Virginia, and the Carolinas fought shoulder to shoulder in western Pennsylvania under Braddock and Forbes. It was then that George Washington won his spurs as a leader.

Although the colonists were generally united in their opposition to the taxes imposed by England, only a minority felt the solution lay in revolution. That is why Dickinson wrote as he did. Most colonists believed that a compromise could still be reached. Franklin himself said, "As between friends every affront is not worth a duel, between nations every injury is not worth a war."

A political battle was going on in Pennsylvania between some who opposed actual revolution against England, many of whom belonged to the upper class, and others who believed revolution was the only answer and struggled for control of the colony's government. The new western counties were not fairly represented in the Assembly, and citizens on the frontier raised the cry of taxation without representation against the government in Philadelphia. The working people of Philadelphia also felt that they had no voice in the Assembly because most of them did not have the right to vote. In order to vote, a man had to own a certain amount of land or other property. These two groups of dissatisfied citizens joined in opposing the Penn government.

The feelings of the frontiersmen spilled over in the winter of 1763–64 when about five hundred of them known as the Paxton Boys from near (later) Harrisburg marched on Philadelphia. Franklin called them "white savages" because they had massacred a number of peaceful Conestoga Indians near Lancaster. These radicals marched all the way to Philadelphia and terrified most of the citizens of the Quaker City. However, Franklin, who was back in Philadelphia, and others persuaded them to return home peacefully after promising them that reforms would be made in the colonial government. It is clear that in Pennsylvania, when the real revolution came along, it was a revolt both against England and the colonial government of the Penns.

It was under these troubled conditions that Great Britain kept trying to enforce its new taxes. Everyone has heard about the Boston Tea Party in which Bostonians threw tea from ships into Boston harbor. Philadelphia had a similar, though not so well-known, tea party. In December, 1773,

An account of the Philadelphia Tea Party.

Captain Ayres, commanding the ship *Polly,* arrived with a cargo of fine tea, and the Philadelphia Sons of Liberty warned the captain that any effort to put his cargo ashore "will most assuredly bring you into hot water." He was also told, "You are sent out on a diabolical service, and if you are so foolish and obstinate as to complete your voyage, by bringing your ship to anchor in this Port, you may run such a Gauntlet as will induce you . . . most heartily to curse those who have made you the Dupe of their Avarice and Ambition." The added threat of a "Halter around your Neck, ten Gallons of liquid Tar . . . with the Feathers of a dozen Geese laid over that to enliven your Appearance" was hardly inviting, and the good Captain Ayres sailed back down the bay without making any effort to land his cargo of tea.

Such was the temper of the times when the First Continental Congress assembled in Philadelphia in Carpenters' Hall on September 4, 1774. Philadelphia was a natural place for the meeting, with its 40,000 people and being the second largest city in the British Empire. The province had offered the State House to the visitors, but the Pennsylvania revolutionary leaders had not yet won control of the local government and did not want the Congress to use it.

The Congress had been called by Massachusetts, where the British attack on the colonies centered. Some of the best information about what went on is in the letters that short, stout, and sometimes bad-tempered John Adams from that colony wrote to his wife, Abigail, at home. He told her about the busy time he was having. "My time is totally filled from the time I get out of bed until I return to it," he wrote.

It was not easy to unite such different interests as those of the southern colonies with those of Puritan Massachusetts. "We have numberless prejudices to remove here," Adams wrote a friend. At one point in the debates at this first Congress, Virginia's fiery Patrick Henry cried out in ringing tones, "The distinctions between Virginians, Pennsylvanians, New Yorkers, and New Englanders are no more. I am not a Virginian but an American." "This was one of the happiest days of my life," wrote John Adams. "This day," he said, "convinced me that America will support Massachusetts." Congress condemned Britain's "Intolerable Acts " and urged Massachusetts to form a new government, refuse to pay British taxes, and arm its militia. The Congress drew up a Declaration of Rights which said among other things that the colonists had such basic rights of Englishmen as "life, liberty, and property" that had not been lost by coming to America. It also created a Continental Association to put an end to import and export trade with England. Having so stated its views, it adjourned on October 26.

Carpenter's Hall was the scene of the First Continental Congress on September 4, 1774, held to debate the question of revolution and independence.

King George III ignored the plea for cherished rights and liberties and declared, "The New England governments are now in a state of rebellion; blows must decide whether they are to be subject to this country or independent." In London Ben Franklin gave up trying to preserve the peace. He sailed for home, but his love of science led him, in spite of the tenseness of the times, to take samples of sea water in an effort to chart the course of the Gulf Stream as his ship sailed over the ocean. England, he said, now seemed to him an "old rotten state." While he was at sea and only halfway home on April 19, 1775, about seventy Massachusetts militiamen traded shots with some seven hundred crack British redcoats at Lexington and Concord. It was a small but violent battle in which there were more than two hundred casualties.

When delegates to the Second Continental Congress returned to Philadelphia on May 10, 1775, the New Englanders were met about six miles outside the city in an outburst of patriotic feeling by "about two hundred of the principal gentlemen, on horseback, with their swords drawn" and later by a "company of riflemen in their uniforms." Silas Deane from Connecticut wrote, "Thus rolling and gathering like a snow ball, we approached the City, which was full of people and the crowd as great as in New York." Bells rang and people cheered. Richard Henry Lee from Virginia was led to remark, "There never appeared more perfect unanimity among any set of men." There were new delegates, among them the wealthy Boston merchant John Hancock, who was to preside and to sign the Declaration of Independence in so bold and flourishing a hand. There was lanky, freckle-faced, sandy-haired Thomas Jefferson, youngest member at thirty-seven, who would write the Declaration of Independence and Colonel George Washington in his brilliant blue and red Virginia militia uniform, "a fine figure and of a most easy and agreeable address." John

Adams was so impressed with Washington in his uniform that he wrote Abigail that he too would like to be a soldier and that he was going to read some military books. One returning member was Philadelphia's Charles Thomson who was re-elected secretary.

There were still those who either were opposed completely to any move for independence from the mother country or wanted to move with great caution. When John Adams urged that Congress ask each colony to form an independent government, he noted that "horror, terror, and detestation, strongly marked the countenances of some of the members." His plea was not heeded, but on June 15 Colonel Washington was placed in command of the Continental Army at Boston, and Congress voted to send ten companies of Maryland, Pennsylvania, and Virginia riflemen to join his army at Boston. A new peace proposal came from Lord North saying if the colonies would take care of their own defense, Parliament would "forbear" from taxing them but would hold on to the "right" to tax them. This was "not a renunciation of the pretended right to tax us," Jefferson wrote for Congress. John Dickinson, who had spoken so strongly in defense of colonial liberties, now declared that if King George III wanted to stop "the effusion of British Blood" he should heed the "Olive Branch" petition Congress had asked him to write. It said the colonists still were loyal to the king and anxious for a peaceful solution to the dispute. This came even after the Battle of Bunker Hill. Radicals like John and Sam Adams were very angry but could do nothing but await events. Sam Adams wrote that "it is very difficult to possess upwards of Sixty Gentlemen at once with the same feelings upon Questions of Importance that are continually arising." Suffering from Philadelphia's hot and humid summer and the flies which swarmed from nearby stables through the open windows into the hall, the delegates on August 2 called a recess until September 12 and the hopefully cooler breezes of autumn.

When Congress came back to Philadelphia the weather was a little cooler and the flies less annoying, but the king had not even answered the Olive Branch petition. Jefferson said this was enough to make separation from England necessary, but as late as December 6 a majority of delegates said they remained loyal to the king but not to Parliament. Something was needed to stir a majority of the colonists to action. It came in the form of a forty-seven page pamphlet called *Common Sense* written by a thirty-eight-year-old English immigrant named Thomas Paine. Benjamin Franklin encouraged him to come to Philadelphia and gave him a letter saying he was an "ingenious, worthy, young man." There Paine met Dr. Benjamin Rush, the noted Philadelphia doctor and leader in the cause of independence, who suggested Paine write such a pamphlet. Although its title was *Common Sense,* it was more of an appeal to emotion. Unlike the writings of men like John Dickinson, it could be understood by the common man. Paine argued for independence not so much by arguing about political ideas but by making fun of "divine right" kings like George III. He said that rule by divine right "certainly hath no divinity in it. . . . One of the strongest natural proofs of the folly of hereditary right in kings, is that nature disapproves it, otherwise she would not so frequently turn it into ridicule by giving mankind an ass for a lion," wrote Paine. "The blood of the slain, the weeping voice of nature cries, 'Tis time to part,' " his fiery pen cried out to the colonists. Within three months of its publication in Philadelphia in January, 1776, it had sold over 100,000 copies.

It seemed as if Parliament's actions were directed to pushing America into declaring independence. In December, 1775, Parliament declared the colonies no longer could

expect the protection of the Crown or the right to trade with England. American ships could even be seized at sea by British warships. Congress in March, 1776, took steps to fit out "armed vessels to cruize on the enemies of these United Colonies," but it would not vote for independence. John Adams wrote that the idea "is a Hobgoblin of so frightful Mien, that it would throw a delicate person into fits to look it in the Face." James Wilson of Pennsylvania rose in Congress to ask, "Before we are prepared to build the new house, why should we tear down the old one?"

Yet the forces of revolution had been set in motion, and in June, 1776, the delegates to the Congress appointed a committee to draft a declaration of independence. The committee that had been appointed to draft this momentous declaration included Benjamin Franklin, John Adams, and Thomas Jefferson. The tall, sandy-haired Jefferson from Vir-

On July 8, 1776, as the Liberty Bell tolled, John Nixon read the Declaration of Independence to an exuberant crowd gathered around the State House.

ginia was not nearly as well known as the elderly Franklin, who had long been famous for his skill with a pen. At first Jefferson tried to get Adams to write the document, but the New Englander told him, "You can write ten times better than I can." Franklin also refused the task, perhaps because he was then very busy doing most of the work writing Pennsylvania's Constitution of 1776 (its first as a new state). Thus Jefferson spent the last three weeks in June working over a draft for the declaration, which finally went to the Congress after only a few changes suggested by Franklin and Adams had been made.

The central statement of the Declaration was, "We hold these truths to be self-evident, that all men are created equal, that they are endowed by their Creator with certain inalienable Rights, that among these are Life, Liberty, and the pursuit of Happiness." Why has this statement had so much influence? It did not express an entirely new idea because the English thinker John Locke had written about the central theme earlier and at great length as a new philosophy of government. But the United States was the first to apply the idea to the creation of a new nation, and it has remained an ideal toward which we continue to strive.

Finally after heated controversy, the Congress voted independence and by July 4, after revising Jefferson's Declaration of Independence, they approved it. On July 8 the Declaration was read to a cheering crowd in the yard of the State House to the accompaniment of the ringing of the Liberty Bell, which was inscribed with the words: "PROCLAIM LIBERTY THROUGHOUT ALL THE LAND UNTO ALL INHABITANTS THEREOF."

In the third column from the left, the first nine signatures are those of Robert Morris, Benjamin Rush, Benjamin Franklin, John Morton, George Clymer, James Smith, George Taylor and James Wilson, who signed the Declaration of Independence on behalf of Pennsylvania.

Bibliography

Many sources were used in writing this book, but this listing is limited to those rather readily available and within the range of the reading ability of those who might be reading this book. Some booklets and leaflets are listed as series to avoid repeating basic information common in single listings and to identify them for easier acquisition.

ANDERSON, NILES. *The Battle of Bushy Run.* Harrisburg, Pa.: History and Museum Commission, 1966 (hereafter cited as PHMC). Twenty-page colorful description of the famous Indian battle.

DOLSON, HILDEGARDE. *William Penn, Quaker Hero.* New York: Random House, 1961.

DONOVAN, FRANK R. *The Many Worlds of Benjamin Franklin.* New York: American Heritage, 1963.

FLETCHER, STEVENSON W. *Pennsylvania Agriculture and Farm Life, 1640–1840.* Harrisburg: PHMC, 1950. More on the life of farm people in colonial days than in any other single book.

HALE, NATHANIEL C. *Pelts and Palisades: The Story of Fur and the Rivalry for Pelts in Early America.* Richmond: The Dietz Press, 1959. Well-written story of the fur trade.

Historic Pennsylvania Leaflets Series. Harrisburg: PHMC. For the colonial period this series contains *Anthony Wayne, The Pennsylvania Rifle, The Conestoga Wagon, The Amish in American Culture, Benjamin Franklin, Col. Henry Bouquet, Young Washington in Pennsylvania, William Penn, The Walking Purchase, Early Painting in Pennsylvania, Conrad Weiser.*

HOSTETLER, JOHN. *Amish Life.* Scottdale, Pa.: Herald Press, 1961.

——— *Mennonite Life.* Scottdale, Pa.: Herald Press, 1961.

JAMES, ALFRED P., and STOTZ, CHARLES M. *Drums in the Forest.* Pittsburgh: Historical Society of Western Pennsylvania, 1958. Good for the western frontier wars and forts telling how they were built and lived in.

KENT, DONALD H. *The French Invasion of Western Pennsylvania.* Harrisburg: PHMC, 1954.

LOVE, NANCY. *Philadelphia Magazine Guide.* Philadelphia: Philadelphia Magazine, 1968. Excellent guide to historic Philadelphia.

Pennsylvania History Studies. University Park: Pennsylvania Historical Association. This series, started in 1948, presents booklets of value which include William W. Comford, *The Quakers;* Russell W. Gilbert, *A Picture of the Pennsylvania Germans;* Ira V. Brown, *Pennsylvania Reformers;* George Swetnam, *Pennsylvania Transportation;* William A. Russ, Jr., *Pennsylvania's Boundaries;* Ira V. Brown, *The Negro in Pennsylvania;* Irwin Richman, *Pennsylvania Architecture.* Those of Brown, Richman, and Swetnam are useful for the colonial period even though wider in scope.

Remember William Penn. Harrisburg: PHMC, 1945. Put together for the tercentenary of Penn's birth and rich in material on Penn and his life.

SPEARE, ELIZABETH G. *Life in Colonial America.* New York: Random House, 1963. Has Pennsylvania material and is written for young people.

TOLLES, FREDERICK W. *Meeting House and Counting House.* Chapel Hill: University of North Carolina Press, 1948. Excellent for Quaker religious and business affairs in colonial times.

WALLACE, PAUL A. W. *Indians in Pennsylvania.* Harrisburg: PHMC, 1964.

——— *Indian Paths of Pennsylvania.* Harrisburg: PHMC, 1965.

——— *Daniel Boone in Pennsylvania.* Harrisburg: PHMC, 1967.

WALLOWER, LUCILLE. *Colonial Pennsylvania.* Camden, N.J.: Thomas Nelson and Sons, 1969. Written mainly for young people.

WASHINGTON, GEORGE. *Journal.* Charlottesville: University of Virginia Press. Fine paperback reproduction of the journal kept by George Washington on his mission to Fort Le Boeuf.

WESLAGER, C. A. *Dutch Explorers, Traders and Settlers on the Delaware, 1609–1664.* Philadelphia: University of Pennsylvania Press, 1961.

WRIGHT, J. E., and CORBETT, DORIS S. *Pioneer Life.* Pittsburgh: University of Pittsburgh. Paperback #41. Excellent and readable, based on Pennsylvania frontier life.

Important Dates

1608—Captain John Smith meets the Susquehannock Indians.

1609—August 28: Henry Hudson in the *Half-Moon* enters Delaware Bay.

1623—The Dutch build Fort Nassau, nearly opposite Philadelphia.

1624—December 21: King Gustavus Adolphus of Sweden authorizes the founding of a colony on the Delaware.

1637—December 31: The ships *Kalmar Nyckel* and *Fogel Grip* set sail from Sweden.

1638—April. Swedish settlements established on the Delaware under Peter Minuit, the first governor of New Sweden.

1643—February 15: Governor Johan Printz establishes his seat of government on Tinicum Island, within the present boundaries of Pennsylvania.

1644—October 24: Birth of William Penn.

1646—First church in Pennsylvania consecrated at Tinicum by the Swedish.

1655—September 15: Governor Johan Rising surrenders New Sweden to Governor Peter Stuyvesant of the New Netherlands.

1664—October 1: Sir Robert Carr takes possession of Delaware settlements for the English.

1673—The Dutch recapture New Netherlands and the Delaware country.

1674—Treaty of peace restores English rule. Sir Edmund Andros, governor.

1676—September 25: Duke of York's laws establish English system of law and justice on the Delaware.

1681—March 4: King Charles II of England signs the charter granting Pennsylvania to William Penn.

—April 2: Proclamation of the charter of Pennsylvania.

—April 10: William Markham commissioned deputy governor.

—August 3: Markham summons Council of nine men to meet at Upland, now Chester. This is the beginning of Pennsylvania's government under the charter.

1682—April: William Penn issues his First Frame of Government.

—October 24: William Penn in the *Welcome* enters Delaware Bay.

—October 28: Philadelphia laid out by Thomas Holme.

—October 29: William Penn lands on Pennsylvania soil at Upland, now Chester.

—December 4: First Pennsylvania Assembly meets at Chester.

—December 7: Great Law enacted by the Assembly.

1683—April 2: Penn and the Assembly agree upon Second Frame of Government.

—August 20: F. D. Pastorius and his colony arrive to found Germantown.

1684—August: William Penn leaves for England.

1688—Protest of Germantown colonists against slavery, first in America.

1689—Friends found a public school in Philadelphia, now William Penn Charter School.

1690—First paper mill in America erected on the Wissahickon by William Rittenhouse.

1692—William Penn deprived of governmental powers over Pennsylvania, and province placed under control of Governor Fletcher of New York.

1694—Penn's governmental powers restored.

1699—William Penn returns to Pennsylvania.

1701—October 25: Penn charters the city of Philadelphia.

—October 28: Penn signs the Charter of Privileges under which Pennsylvania was governed until the Revolution.

1701—Penn returns to England.

1703—Lower Counties, now State of Delaware, sever connections with Pennsylvania, and set up separate Assembly.

1716—First ironworks established on Manatawney Creek, Berks County, by Thomas Rutter.

1718—July 30: William Penn dies in England, at the age of seventy-four.

1719—December 22: Andrew Bradford publishes first issue of *American Weekly Mercury,* first newspaper in the middle colonies, and third in the British colonies in North America.

1723—October: Benjamin Franklin arrives in Philadelphia, a friendless boy.

1731—Library Company of Philadelphia is founded, the first such institution in this country.

1740—Foundation of charity school which grew into University of Pennsylvania.

1741—February: The first American magazine published in Philadelphia.

1742—First American singing society established in Bethlehem.

1743—American Philosophical Society founded in Philadelphia.

1748—November: James Hamilton becomes governor of Pennsylvania, the first of American birth.

1751—May 11: Pennsylvania Hospital in Philadelphia chartered, the oldest in the United States.

1752—March 25: First insurance company in America chartered, the Philadelphia Contributionship for the Insurance of Houses from Loss by Fire.

 —June 15: Franklin demonstrates the identity of lightning and electricity.

1753—May: French Force under Boishebert lands at present Erie, and begins Fort Presque Isle.

 —July: French army under Marin builds Fort Le Boeuf (at Waterford).

 —December 11: George Washington reaches Fort Le Boeuf, bearing warning messages to French from the governor of Virginia.

1754—April 17: French under Contrecoeur capture William Trent's fort at the forks of the Ohio, now Pittsburgh, and begin to build Fort Duquesne.

 —July 4: Washington surrenders Fort Necessity to French under de Villiers.

1755—July 9: Defeat of General Braddock by the French and Indians at the Battle of the Monongahela.

 —October 16: First Indian massacres at Penn's Creek begin period of Indian raids on the frontier.

1758—November 28: Expedition of General John Forbes occupies ruins of Fort Duquesne, renamed Pittsburgh in honor of Prime Minister William Pitt.

1763—May 9: Pontiac's War begins, when Indians besiege Detroit.

—June: Indians attack forts in western Pennsylvania, destroying Forts Presque Isle, Le Boeuf and Venango. Fort Pitt besieged.

—August 5–6: Colonel Henry Bouquet defeats Indians at Bushy Run, raising siege of Fort Pitt.

—December 30: Mason and Dixon began survey of Pennsylvania-Maryland boundary.

1765—The College of Philadelphia opens the first medical school in the country, now the Department of Medicine of the University of Pennsylvania.

—November 7: Merchants of Philadelphia protest against the Stamp Act.

1767–68—John Dickinson writes *Letters of a Pennsylvania Farmer.*

1768—July 30: Nonimportation resolutions adopted by Philadelphia mass meeting at the State House.

1769—June 3: Transit of Venus observed by Rittenhouse.

—Connecticut men make first permanent settlement in the Wyoming Valley, resulting in the Yankee-Pennamite Wars.

1774—May 19: Paul Revere arrives in Philadelphia to urge Pennsylvanians to support the cause of Boston.

—September 5: First Continental Congress meets in Carpenters' Hall, Philadelphia.

1775—May 10: Second Continental Congress meets in the State House, Philadelphia.

—June 15: Washington appointed commander in chief in Philadelphia.

—June 30: Pennsylvania Committee of Safety formed.

—July 19: *Experiment* launched, first boat of Pennsylvania Navy.

1776—June 18: Provincial conference of county committees of correspondence calls convention to make state constitution.

—July 4: Declaration of Independence adopted.

—August 2: Declaration of Independence signed.

Places To Visit

There are so many historic sites in Pennsylvania, it is impossible to list more than a sample of those of major importance. Space does not permit listing visiting hours but almost all are open every day from about 9 A.M. to 5 P.M. Historic sites under the Pennsylvania Historical and Museum Commission in Harrisburg are listed as PHMC. Children are admitted free. A Trail of History map is available showing all of these. Special folders on each may be obtained from the commission and the same is true of National Park Service areas. A listing of all state historical markers with location and inscriptions is in the *Guide to Historical Markers of Pennsylvania* and may be obtained from the Pennsylvania Historical and Museum Commission, Harrisburg. The *Philadelphia Magazine Guide* published by the *Philadelphia Magazine* and the *Bulletin Almanac* published by the Philadelphia *Evening Bulletin* are very useful for the location of the multitude of historic places in the city. Group visits should be arranged in advance. A general listing follows.

BETHLEHEM. A group called Historic Bethlehem, Inc., is restoring the old Moravian church and other buildings in this city. It is the most complete restoration of a group of colonial buildings in any one city.

BRANDYWINE BATTLEFIELD STATE PARK. Near Greensburg and Jeannette on Pennsylvania 993. Site of Colonel Bouquet's defeat of the Indians in 1763. Park area and small modern museum. PHMC.

CALEB PUSEY HOUSE. Race Street, Chester. Restoration of the oldest house in Pennsylvania with other buildings.

CONRAD WEISER PARK. East of Womelsdorf on U. S. 422. Home of the great Indian interpreter and peacemaker. Small park and museum. PHMC.

CORNWALL FURNACE. At Cornwall on U. S. 322. Ironworks dating back over two centuries and museum. Nearby are the Cornwall ore banks used since about 1740 as a source of iron ore. PHMC.

DANIEL BOONE HOMESTEAD. Near Reading off U. S. 422. Restored home of Boone, restored log cabin of Boone era and Museum of the Pennsylvania Pioneer. PHMC.

FORT AUGUSTA. Site of Fort Augusta at Sunbury with scale replica and museum. PHMC.

FORT LE BOEUF MEMORIAL. U. S. 19 near Erie. Site of French fort at Waterford. Museum and monument to George Washington. PHMC.

FORT LIGONIER. On U. S. 30 at Ligonier. Probably the finest restored fort anywhere and excellent museum under the Fort Ligonier Association.

FORT NECESSITY NATIONAL HISTORIC SITE. Near Uniontown on U. S. 40. Restored fort and museum where the French and Indian War started. Remains of the Braddock Road and Braddock's Grave are nearby; also Jumonville Glenn where Washington had his first skirmish with the French.

FORT PITT. Excavated ruins of the walls of Fort Pitt and outlines of main bastions, marked location of French Fort Duquesne, the original Fort Pitt Blockhouse, and the new and modern Fort Pitt Museum are all within the confines of Point State Park at the junction of the Monongahela and Allegheny in downtown Pittsburgh.

GERMANTOWN IN PHILADELPHIA. Germantown has many places of historic importance dating to the colonial era. These include Cliveden which was a center of the Battle of Germantown, Wyck, Bechtel House, Green Tree Tavern, Grumblethorpe, Germantown Academy, David James Dove House, Johnson House, Church of Brethren, Mennonite Meeting House, and Stenton, home of James Logan, all built before the Revolution and preserved or restored.

HOPE LODGE. Near Fort Washington and Pennsylvania Turnpike interchange 26. Colonial mansion. PHMC.

HOPEWELL VILLAGE NATIONAL HISTORIC SITE. At Elverson near Pennsylvania Turnpike interchange 22. Restoration of colonial iron furnace and mansion dating to 1770.

INDEPENDENCE NATIONAL HISTORIC PARK. This park covers nearly five acres and has in its limits Independence Hall. Nearby is Carpenters' Hall still owned by the Carpenters Company.

PENNSBURY MANOR. Near Morrisville and Bristol off U. S. 1 and

13. Re-created manor house and outbuildings and Penn's barge which were Penn's country home on his second visit. Not far distant is historic Fallsington, a restored Quaker village of Penn's time.

PHILADELPHIA. The city is full of great landmarks. Fairmount Park has in its limits Lemon Hill, Robert Morris' home, Mt. Pleasant, Ormiston, The Randolph Mansion, Woodford, Strawberry Mansion, and Cedar Grove, all colonial mansions. Buildings which today house the Library Company of Philadelphia, The Pennsylvania Hospital, and the American Philosophical Society, all firsts in America, have art, documents, and other material illustrating the colonial era. Historic churches in lower Philadelphia include "Old Pine" Presbyterian, Old St. Joseph's Catholic, St. Peter's, and St. Paul's. The last two are historic Episcopal churches. Old St. George's Methodist was started in 1763. Gloria Dei (Old Swedes' Church), the oldest and most famous Christ Church building, dates back to 1727. The *Guide* and the *Bulletin Almanac* should be used for further information.

POTTSGROVE. At Pottsgrove on U. S. 422. Restored home of a colonial ironmaster, John Potts, and beautifully furnished. PHMC.

MUSEUMS

AMERICAN SWEDISH HISTORICAL MUSEUM. 1900 Pattison Avenue, Philadelphia. Material on the history of the Swedes in Pennsylvania.

ANNIE S. KEMERER MUSEUM. Bethlehem at Main and Church streets. Early Bethlehem things, and on the same street is the Moravian Museum with early Moravian artifacts.

HISTORICAL SOCIETY OF BERKS COUNTY. 940 Center Avenue, Reading. Early Reading history.

CHESTER COUNTY HISTORICAL SOCIETY. West Chester. Excellent things in the way of early furniture, glass, and so forth.

ELFRETH'S ALLEY ASSOCIATION. At 126 Elfreth's Alley, Philadelphia. The association has a museum of colonial Philadelphia and there is also the oldest street in Philadelphia much as it was in colonial days.

HERSHEY MUSEUM. At Hershey and contains in a general museum Indian artifacts, Stiegel glass, and other early items.

THE HISTORICAL SOCIETY OF PENNSYLVANIA. At 1300 Locust Street in Philadelphia. Has a fine collection of portraits and other things relating to William Penn and Franklin.

HISTORICAL SOCIETY OF YORK COUNTY. 250 Market Street, York. Excellent museum displays on early York.

LYCOMING HISTORICAL SOCIETY. 405 West Third Street, Williamsport. Excellent new museum with Indian artifacts and a working grist mill.

MARITIME MUSEUM. 427 Chestnut Street, Philadelphia. The finest museum on early Philadelphia shipping and maritime history.

MERCER MUSEUM. Pine and Ashland streets in Doylestown. Tools, implements, and machinery before the age of steam. Operated by the Bucks County Historical Society.

PENNSYLVANIA ACADEMY OF THE FINE ARTS. At Broad and Cherry streets in Philadelphia and one of the finest collections of early American art.

PENNSYLVANIA FARM MUSEUM. At Landis Valley near Lancaster. Outstanding collection and buildings on Pennsylvania farm life, tools, implements, and folk art. PHMC.

PENNSYLVANIA MILITARY MUSEUM. At Boalsburg near State College. General military museum but goes back to colonial military history. PHMC.

PHILADELPHIA MUSEUM OF ART. Twenty-sixth Street and Benjamin Franklin Parkway, Philadelphia. Noteworthy for period rooms and outstanding collection of Pennsylvania German things.

WILLIAM PENN MEMORIAL MUSEUM. Harrisburg. The state museum and exhibits include colonial life. PHMC.

WYOMING HISTORICAL AND GEOLOGICAL SOCIETY. 69 South Franklin Street, Wilkes-Barre. Notable for Indian artifacts and early Wilkes-Barre history.

Index

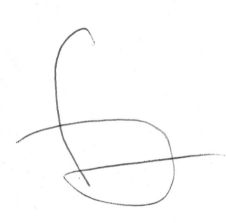